Siiri Reimann
Aime Edasi

The Haapsalu Shawl

A Knitted Lace Tradition from Estonia

Saara Publishing House
2009

Siiri Reimann, Aime Edasi
THE HAAPSALU SHAWL
A Knitted Lace Tradition from Estonia
Translation: Maret Tamjärv

Compiling of this book was assisted by Marju Heldema
Introduction: Aidi Vallik
Editor: Anu Pink
Consultant and editor of the English edition: Nancy Bush
Cover design: Mariann Einmaa
Interior design: Mariann Einmaa
Photo credits: Atko Januson, Anu Pink, Läänemaa Museum, Estonian National Museum, President's Office, Tõnis Padu,
private collections
Drawings: Ülle Kuldkepp
Figures and schemes: Siiri Reimann

We thank the master knitters of Haapsalu who made samples and shawls for this book and contributed their knowledge
to this book:
Linda Elgas, Maiva Dunkel, Saima Tee, Helga Rüütel, Laine Põldme, Silvi Saarlo, Helmi Mändla, Viivi Palmiste, Miralda Piper,
Mall Kütt, Malle Yeremeyeva, Elgi Simulask, Aasa Jõelaid, Tiia Kaus, Ruth Bormann, Mirje Sims, Elfride Ohtla, Marta Kumari,
Aive Ploom, Ly Härm, Aime Saareleht.

We thank the fair ladies who model the shawls in this book, and the Läänemaa Museum for assistance in composing the historical
information.

Saara Publishing House
Vabriku 1, Türi, Estonia
www.saara.ee

ISBN 978-9985-9925-9-3
© Saara kirjastus 2009
© Siiri Reimann, Aime Edasi 2009

Help with the publishing of this book has been contributed by:
Estonian Culture Endowment, Local Self-Initiative Programme, Haapsalu City Government, Läänemaa expert group of Estonian
Culture Endowment, Läänemaa Artisans' Union, Movek Grupp, Haapsalu Door Factory, LLC Tradilo, Est-Trans Kaubaveod Ltd.

Haapsalu, located on the shore of the Baltic Sea, is a small Estonian town which received town bylaws in 1279. Being surrounded by the sea on three sides, this quiet town is known as a health resort with curative mud. It is also famous for its medieval Episcopal Castle, a dwelling place of the most celebrated ghost of Estonia, THE WHITE LADY.

On dark August nights the White Lady reveals herself in the baptistery window of the Episcopal Castle. Legend has it that a maiden of Estonian blood was walled alive into the half-finished wall of the baptistery as, though forbidden, she had continued to live in sin with one of the canons. The poor woman's soul couldn't find peace and thus, for centuries, she appears in the baptistery window to prove the immortality of her love.

About the same amount of recognition has been brought to Haapsalu by its hand-knit lacy scarves and shawls. One often speaks about delicate Haapsalu lace shawls, yet what this airy needlecraft really is about, what makes it different from other lacy shawls and how to knit them – these are the questions frequently put to knitters of Haapsalu.

With this book we hope to introduce the culture of the Haapsalu shawl to a wider audience and encourage anyone interested in handicraft to try out shawl knitting. Although at the beginning, knitting a Haapsalu shawl may seem complicated, the joy from a hand-knit, airy shawl soon makes up for all the pains taken. In the course of working, it will appear that it is not that difficult at all.

The tradition of the Haapsalu shawl and the town which has given the name to this tradition are inseparable. Therefore, together with the shawls, we will try to introduce you to the atmosphere of this small town as well as its celebrated ladies.

Kind reader and handicraft lover, the book you are holding in your hand has captured the secrets of the Haapsalu shawl and there is nothing left but hope that you, too, will enjoy knitting these lovely shawls as much as we do.

Siiri and Aime from Haapsalu

Estonia, Haapsalu

Contents

Haapsalu and the Shawl

Haapsalu abounds with fresh air and gentleness. The houses are small and low, almost as if intended for dolls. Foliage of trees spreads its green lace above the rooftops. Sunny courtyards, dozing in the lap of bushes and flower beds, have looked nearly the same for more than a century: half-hidden behind board fences from the eyes of strollers in the street. The scenery is not weighty; behind those shrubs, ancient trees and courtyards, one can feel a vast expanse, the sea sparkles in the distance, beyond the boundary of the streets. And there is wind, there is wind most all the time.

The shawl could not develop in an empty place for no particular reason, be born out of nothing. Refined guests from St. Petersburg visited also other places, not only Haapsalu; much more Russian handiwork should have reached bigger towns, larger cities which had Russian officials and teachers as residents. Yet no, it was just here that houses were decorated with wooden lace and the delicate and cobwebby Haapsalu shawl started to draw away from original, early examples and live a life of its own.

It seems that the shawl had to fit here, to express something substantial and familiar about this place. The heart of Haapsalu does not lie between the castle walls, although many a man from the ancient past or present would like to think so. Quite the contrary, it is the small-sized and dollish houses and streets of the old town that make Haapsalu – open to the sea, vast on three sides – into a safe and warm place, just like the finest wool yarn makes warm airy patterns.

The strange regularity, as if at odds with natural law, is that in Haapsalu there is more inside than outside. I don't know how this can be possible, but houses that seem tiny to the eye from outside turn out to be spacious and high when you step inside; the short end of a street, running to the sea, gives the impression of a long walk, and the inner world of a simple commonplace man displays the whole cosmos – if only you can get close enough and are

admitted to discover it. The same applies to the Haapsalu shawl – if you haven't tried it yourself, you would never believe that this relatively small-sized lace shawl could be warm. But when you take it close and spread it proudly on your shoulders, all of a sudden you realize that it is not merely lace or a piece of peacockish finery. Much more, it is warm and safe, airy and delicate, loose and closed at the same time, such a peculiar shawl. Just like Haapsalu itself.

And like the shawl, some parts of the town, too, have remained in the late 1800's, the idyllic pre-war time when the cruelty and chaos of the 20th century was still unimaginable and neither the media nor cars rushed the daily tempo of life. Surely nowadays many a stressed soul sometimes thinks of these lost times and lets his spirit be touched by a vague craving for this tranquillity and slow course. And even if we never get back these times – another matter is the rational question: do we really want this, as modern life still has its advantages --, then at least together with the air of Haapsalu we can breathe in the past atmosphere. Let us be carried by soothing mental pictures of these bygone times and enter games of fantasy in almost every street and courtyard of the old town, on the promenade, in the New Harbor, the Count's Garden as well as by the Viik (a shallow bay). At every step we are supported by mild and quieting history which makes our own personal life and all its problems withdraw to something smaller and less important.

Then it may happen that, instead of a jacket to cover our shoulders, we would be grateful for a Haapsalu shawl – a reminder of the time when women were more indulged and had more time to be a weaker vessel; from the time when big wars and globalization were still part of science fiction; from the time of idyllic peace and quiet which allowed everyone to be a little more their own person.

Aidi Vallik
writer from Haapsalu

The History of the Haapsalu Shawl

Different sources suggest several versions concerning the beginning of the lace knitting tradition in Haapsalu. One legend tells that knitting of these shawls originated from an Estonian Swedish family who settled in Haapsalu in the second quarter of the 19th century. According to another legend, the interest in knitting shawls was spread in Haapsalu by women of Vormsi, a small island in the Baltic Sea. Yet some authorities insist that inspiration came from Orenburg and Penza lace scarves brought to the town by Russian holiday-makers.

The wives of free farmers and artisans who had moved into Haapsalu in the 19th century, searched for the opportunity to continue making handicraft in urban conditions. Since town houses were small, there was no room for weaving looms. Industrious and creative women started to make scarves and shawls by hand knitting. At first these hand-knit shawls had simple patterns and were mostly black, white or grey striped, but after some time they started to be worked in lacy patterns.

When, in 1825, Dr. Carl Abraham Hunnius founded the first mud therapy institution in Haapsalu, a pivotal event occurred for the whole town. Because of this mud bath, wealthy Russian gentlefolk began visiting the small town and Haapsalu developed into a health resort. With the increasing demand, many bathing establishments were built which, in summertime, attracted aristocracy from St. Petersburg and Moscow, including the imperial family of Russia. Owing to wealthy vacationers the handicraft created by Haapsalu women found many buyers.

View of the Kurhaus and Mud Baths, early 20th century.

The Russian heir to the throne Tsarevitch Alexander with his family and court in front of De la Gardie's Castle in Haapsalu, 1880.

There is a legend, still famous today in Haapsalu, about a party held in 1859 at De la Gardie's Castle on the name day of the Russian Empress. Two thousand guests had been invited and music was played by an orchestra from Riga. The Empress was presented with a cobwebby shawl packed in a coconut shell. When the shawl was spread out, it veiled the lady from head to toe. Such beautiful delicate shawls which complimented fine dresses became desirable for many noble ladies.

Beginning in 1845, in the summertime, a steamer sailed regularly between St. Petersburg, Tallinn, Haapsalu and Riga. Women's needlecraft was often taken to the ships stopping in Haapsalu, and many bulk purchases of scarves and shawls were made, to be resold later. In this way the Haapsalu scarves and shawls travelled to other cities besides St. Petersburg and Moscow.

Passenger steamer in Haapsalu harbor

Haapsalu railway station in about 1910

The railway line, completed in 1905, further improved the connection with the resort and gave fresh energy to the town's enterprise. During the best summer seasons, the number of tourists reached close to 4000; hotels of Haapsalu filled up, various new cafes were opened and social activities became more lively. More opportunities were available for selling handicraft completed during the winter months.

St. Petersburg Hotel in Haapsalu, early 20th century

By the end of the 19th century shawl knitting became an essential source of additional income for many families. At the height of lace knitting in the late 19th – early 20th centuries some families completed about seventy or eighty scarves and shawls during the winter. All female family members were engaged in knitting. Girls were taught to knit at an early age – often as young as the age of seven – in some families, even young boys helped with the knitting.

On summer evenings the knitters of Haapsalu would gather on the promenade, sitting on benches, knitting and selling their shawls from baskets beside them. Busy working women were attractive to vacationers and their warm knitwear sold well on chilly evenings.

Knitting and selling of wool scarves on the promenade in the shade of a board fence behind the trees, August 1933.

Concert on the promenade

Lace knitting, having declined during the First World War (1914–1918), began once again when Estonia became an independent republic. The Haapsalu city government advertised the town as a resort known for its curative mud and delicate scarves. Once again Haapsalu became a destination for holiday-makers. Instead of Russian gentlefolk it was now tourists from Finland, Sweden and other European countries who arrived in Haapsalu. Along with foreigners, this quiet small town also attracted Estonia's own vacationers. It was easy for them to visit the resort by traveling on the Tallinn-Haapsalu train. The opportunity of selling handicraft, the well-known Haapsalu scarves and shawls, opened up again.

When the town received honorable guests, the Haapsalu shawl often served as a souvenir and gift. Thus, the then Crown Prince and later King of Sweden, Gustav Adolf, was given a scarf when he called at Haapsalu during his visit to Estonia in 1932.

Holiday-makers on the promenade.
On the background, Dr. Arronet Mud Baths (with a chimney)
and a plane having arrived from Finland.

Maret Sõerd, employee of the Haapsalu city government, helped the knitters find prospects for introducing and selling lace shawls outside Estonia. Within several years negotiations were held with the director of the Alex Lee Wallau department store in New York in hope of employing 400–500 women who could have lived on lace knitting. This plan was interrupted by the Second World War (1939–1945) and the political and social changes that followed.

Agents of the United States companies and mayor Dr. Hans Alver inspecting the handicraft of Haapsalu, 1938.

Haapsalu scarves and shawls were successfully displayed in numerous handicraft exhibitions, including the shows of 1936 in New York and 1938 in Berlin. Thanks to both of these exhibitions and also tourists, the lacy scarves gained recognition and people in the Scandinavian countries, Germany, England, Canada and elsewhere became interested in purchasing them. One order was even placed from Northern Africa.

Several acknowledged entrepreneurs were among the local master knitters. One of them was Anette Martson, a noteworthy master who had about fifty women knitting for her and who received more than thirty awards for her scarves and shawls.

The highest award won by A. Martson from the agricultural show of Tallinn Estonian Farmers' Sociey in 1936

Acclaimed knitter Anette Martson together with her students in 1913.

Anette Martson would purchase a large quantity of yarn and distribute it among the knitters. The knitters gave their completed work back to her and Mrs Martson finished the shawls by washing and blocking them. She also organized their sales.

Another well-known employer was Ms Grünewald from the German community who had also some twenty or thirty knitters working for her. Most of their production was taken to Leipzig and Bremen in Germany.

The master knitters started to share their experience with students. Courses of lace knitting were taught at the handicraft department of Haapsalu School of Domestic Economy.

The tradition of lace knitting almost vanished due to the Second World War and the following Soviet occupation. In the 1950s, owing to the existing older masters and the strong tradition, a local association of knitters with disabilities and the Haapsalu Industrial and Service Enterprise were formed. Besides other handicraft items they also knitted Haapsalu scarves and shawls.

The slogan „This year more than yesteryear!" was typical during the Soviet period as the demand and market of the Soviet Union were enormous. Shawl knitters worked at home and had to deliver their completed work to the enterprise on certain days. The monthly quota was either nine scarves, or twelve shawls, the size of which had been reduced for maximum profit.

By the 1960s it became impossible to fulfill the ever-increasing demand of the vast Russian market by hand knitting. Thus, center sections of the shawls began to be made by the MEDA knitting machine. Work was carried out in three shifts. The patterns became ever more simple, the shawls were shorter and only the lace edges were made by hand. On some shawls even the lace edging was discontinued and replaced by fringe at the ends. According to Silvi Saarloo this marked the decline of Haapsalu shawls.

This decline ended, in November, 1966 with the beginning of the Haapsalu branch of UKU craft cooperative. It was initiated by Haapsalu handicraft teacher, Leili Leht, who organized seventy or eighty women to work at the cooperative.

The best and most experienced lace knitters were employed at UKU, where shawls and scarves were again knitted following the old traditions.

Lace knitters of UKU craft cooperative in the 1980s: master Irene Kaljas, controller of technical quality, Ilme Sintal, and knitter, accountant and, later master knitter, Maiva Dunkel.

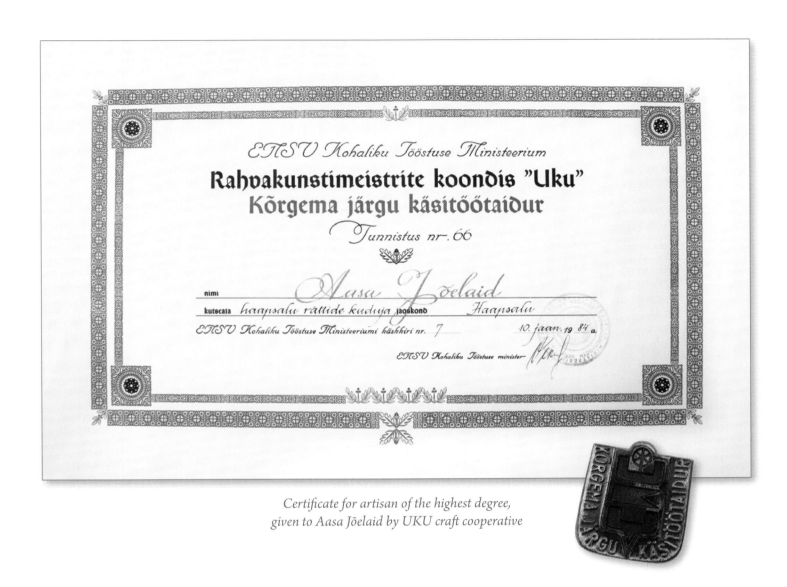

Certificate for artisan of the highest degree,
given to Aasa Jõelaid by UKU craft cooperative

Incorporation of the textured technique called *nupp* (button or bobble) in the shawl was in demand more often as this was proof that a shawl was hand-knitted. Alas, it was impossible to make *nupp*s by the MEDA knitting machine.

This was the beginning of a new dawn for Haapsalu shawls. There was a big demand for knitters and, as well as the contributors to UKU, many other women started to knit shawls in the evening apart their main occupations.

The size and weight of each shawl was strictly dictated and constantly checked. Shawls were taken to the central store in Tallinn and often resold to other republics of the Soviet Union. Eventually it became impossible to buy a shawl in its native town, Haapsalu.

Work of the best knitters was presented for evaluation to the commission of the Tallinn branch of UKU which gave out certificates determining the skill level of a knitter. The knitters of Haapsalu often received certificates of the highest degree for their beautiful shawls.

The handiwork of UKU knitters was so highly appreciated that during the Soviet occupation when Estonians were deprived of the possibility of travel and movement outside Estonia's borders, the shawls could still travel freely about the world. Haapsalu shawls were displayed in exhibitions all over the world. For example, in 1967, shawls by Linda Elgas and Ester Nilpi were sent to the World's Fair in Montreal. In the same year Ester Nilpi's shawl was displayed in the Exhibition of Achievements of the National Economy in Moscow.

In 1970 a shawl by Tiia Nilpi (Kangur) was exhibited at the Osaka World's Fair and in 1976, one of Linda Elgas' shawls was displayed in Paris.

Lace knitters were subservient to the UKU craft cooperative until the early 1990s. In 1991 the Republic of Estonia regained its independence. The change of politics brought changes in all walks of life. Vilta handicraft enterprise was founded; it operated for a short period after UKU was closed and gave work to several shawl knitters. Since both above-mentioned handicraft companies ceased to operate, the masters themselves have had to organize the sale of their own shawls.

In 1992 the Haapsalu Handicraft Society was founded, which carries on past handicraft traditions and brings together many currently active lace knitters.

In order to preserve the tradition of the Haapsalu shawl and scarf, in 1997, the Haapsalu Handicraft Society in partnership with the Central Society of Estonian Home Industry Development organized a conference dedicated to the Haapsalu shawl. Asta Veenpere, researcher at the local museum, lectured about the history of the shawl and, Silvi Saarlo introduced the activities of master knitters. The tradition of the Days of Haapsalu Shawl was initiated in the same year. Since 1999 this event also incorporates a knitting competition held at the Kurhaus, a historic building on the promenade, where those interested in knitting can compete in working shawl patterns.

The first competition of knitting shawls in the Kurhaus in 1999

Beginning in 2008 the sale of shawls was encouraged by handsome packaging that simply invites one to buy.

The Haapsalu Handicraft Society contributed to a collection of scarf patterns by Linda Elgas, „Haapsalu Scarves" (*Haapsalu rätikud*), which was published in 2001. The book contains twenty beautiful scarf patterns with corresponding photos.

Linda Elgas is an extremely creative and fruitful knitter who has completed more than 1000 scarves and shawls. She has organized personal exhibitions, her knitwear has been displayed and won recognition at several competitions in different countries. In 2001 Linda Elgas was awarded the title of Estonian Heritage Keeper. In the course of many years she has passed on her knowledge and skills to her numerous students.

The appeal from 2007, „Ladies, knitters of shawls, contact us!", was answered by 34 people. Today half of them have joined the Haapsalu Handicraft Society. The society encourages the knitting of Haapsalu scarves and shawls, teaching courses of knitting as well as participating in the artisans' meetings and exhibitions. Two biggest endeavors of the past few years have been a display in the Estonian Handicraft House, Tallinn, and a traveling exhibition in Finland in connection with the 90th anniversary of the Republic of Estonia. Haapsalu shawls were displayed in Finnish towns for ten months.

Master knitter Linda Elgas

All these projects have been possible thanks to the good knitters. Why have these masters knitted and why do they still knit, if completing a shawl is such a big and time-consuming task? Habit might serve as one of the reasons. If you have knitted your whole life, then you just cannot live without it. Lace knitting also provides an additional income which is also important. Fortunately today there is a flourishing market for lace shawls in Haapsalu. Shawls and scarves are sold by the local handicraft and art shops, such as Ehte Käsitöö, Kunstikoda, Marimirt and Gift. Due to the small number of master knitters the demand for finished scarves and shawls is larger than the supply. There is also a big demand for shawls outside Haapsalu.

Masters of the Haapsalu Handicraft Society

Haapsalu scarves and shawls have gone through better and worse times. Once the lace shawl was the height of fashion, and later, out of fashion, but it has always been held in great esteem in Haapsalu. Just like the local curative mud and the legend of the White Lady, the Haapsalu shawl, too, has been considered as something permanent and unmistakable. Today hand-knit lace is in fashion again and many people take interest in knitting and wearing it.

Courses of knitting a Haapsalu shawl are taught at Haapsalu High School and Haapsalu Center of Vo-cational Education. There is hope that thanks to the youth who have studied the secrets of the Haapsalu shawl, the tradition will be carried on just in the same way it has reached us through hardships from the past two hundred years.

We hope that, with the help of the following instructions, those who would like to wear a warm lace shawl will be encouraged to try out lace knitting. A homemade shawl is surely the best and the most beautiful.

Master knitters from the late 19th century. A. Amberg, H. Lao, I. Tammik, L. Tamberg, A. Klems and K. Kõrv

Top photo: today's masters Helmi Mändla, Laine Põldme, Linda Elgas, Aime Edasi, Viivi Palmiste and Miralda Piper
Bottom photo: future masters Klaudia-Karmen Sinisalu, Hanna-Liis Lao, Pille-Riin Lusik, Liisi Leier, Silvia Ladva and Kertu Simulask from Haapsalu High School

Teaching the Traditions of a Haapsalu Shawl

The tradition of hand knitted Haapsalu shawls with their distinctive techniques has endured for one and a half centuries. The skill has been handed down from one generation to the next. Mothers and grandmothers taught their daughters (and sometimes also sons) to knit as early as the age of seven or eight.

Three generations of knitters: grandmother Anna Randes, mother Helene Peimann and daughter Niina Gerrez (Gerretz).
There were numerous knitters' families of this kind in Haapsalu.

Later on, new knitters were taught by knitting masters and entrepreneurs in order to guarantee the use of correct methods in knitting the Haapsalu shawl. During the period of UKU craft cooperative from 1966 until the early 1990s, the teaching of lace knitting was organized in Haapsalu and elsewhere. However, at all times the technical details and secrets of shawl knitting have been passed on among family and friends from hand to hand.

In this way the traditional methods of knitting a Haapsalu shawl have reached the present time. Today's master knitters Linda Elgas, Aime Edasi, Maiva Dunkel, Helmi Mändla and Viivi Palmiste have kindly shared their knowledge and experience of lace knitting which is presented in this book as Master's advice.

In the 1970s–1980s, for training new knitters, the „Program of the school of progressive methods of work for knitters of the Haapsalu shawl" was developed in the Haapsalu branch of UKU.

KINNITAN
RMK "UKU" peainsener
.... K.Riive
„..." april 1980.a.

Haapsalu rätiku kudujate
eesrindlike töömeetodite kooli
programm

Kooli eesmärk: toodangu kvaliteedi tõstmine.

Haapsalu salli ja rätiku kudujate eesrindlike
töömeetodite kooli õppuste temaatiline plaan

Jrk. nr.	Teema	Tundide arv
1	2	3
1.	Eesrindlike töömeetodite kooli eesmärk	2 t.
2.	Nõuded toodangu kvaliteedile, esinenud puudused ja selle põhjused	2 t.
3.	Ratsionaalne silmade arvestus ja viimistlus	4 t.
4.	Ratsionaalse arvestuse õpetamine:	
	a) haapsalu salli silmuste arvutamine näidete põhjal	3 t.

Yarns

In most cases Haapsalu shawls are knitted of white yarn. Historically natural black and grey yarn have also been used, along with natural white lambs wool. In the mid-19th century, in order for the shawl to be miraculously fine and soft, yarn was spun from wool from the back of young sheep. Later, fine, high-quality yarn began to be imported from abroad. In the early 20th century yarn was available from Sweden, England and Latvia. During the first years of the Republic of Estonia (1918–1940) the knitters valued the high-quality yarn imported from England; later, fine yarn was mostly obtained from Ogre, Latvia. Even today the lace knitters of Haapsalu still use yarn produced in Ogre, as well as yarn from Estonia, Sweden, Germany, etc.

Nowadays colored Haapsalu shawls are also knitted along with the classical white shawls, but they still have to be made from fine wool yarn.

- *The shawl is usually knitted from soft, fine two-ply wool yarn. Single lambs wool yarn is also suitable, although knitting a shawl and sewing on the lace edge is more complicated, as this yarn tends to break easily. Fine merino yarn is also used.*

- *Depending on the size, pattern, thickness of yarn and tension of knitting, about 70–100g of yarn should be calculated for one shawl. The average yarn has about 1,400 meters (1,100 yards) in 100 grams.*

Master's advice

If the yarn breaks during knitting, tie a knot, as shown in the picture, leaving about 10 cm (4 in.) long ends.

In further working, weave in both strands – one of them before the knot and the other behind it.

The knot is less visible
- *in a nupp*
- *in the garter-stitch frame surrounding the center section*

Knitting Tools

Needles

Haapsalu master knitters work with short (15–20 cm, 6–8 in.) single-point wood needles.
Traditionally, the knitters used strong and smooth needles hand-carved from apple or lilac wood.
In Haapsalu needles are also known to be made of bone.
Nowadays both wood and bamboo needles are used.

Master knitter Aasa Jõelaid's needles carved from a bamboo ski pole

Apple wood needles owned by master knitter Maiva Dunkel

Lilac wood needles owned by master knitter Linda Elgas

Master's advice

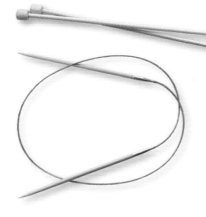

If short wood needles can't be easily found, they can be made at home by glueing wood beads to one end of bamboo double-pointed needles.

The usual needle size is No 3–3.5 mm (US 2½ - 4), this being determined by the thickness of the yarn and tension of the individual knitter.

It is important to make sure that the knitted fabric will be delicate and loose.

To cast on, one needs needles one size larger than will be used for the body of the shawl, so that during blocking, the cast-on edge of the shawl will stretch as much as the openwork center and the bind-off.

For knitting the lace edge of a Haapsalu shawl it is recommended to use longer wood needles or circular bamboo needles.

Frame

In finishing a Haapsalu shawl, an adjustable frame is used on which the wet shawl is blocked and air-dried.

The frame consists of four wooden boards tied together at the corners at a distance determined by the size of the shawl.

The frame has wooden pegs or stainless steel nails onto which the shawl is mounted at each point on the lace edge.

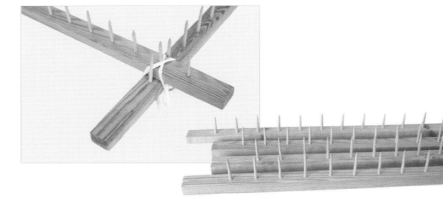

Haapsalu Shawl

A Haapsalu shawl is always rectangular.

The average shawl measures about:
60–70 cm (24–28 in.) or 115–140 stitches **wide**
170–180 cm (66–70 in.) or 220–230 garter-stitch ridges **long**.

In knitting a shawl smaller or bigger than the regular size you should plan for a proportion of 1: 3 – for instance, 60 cm (24 in.) wide by 180 cm (72 in.) long.

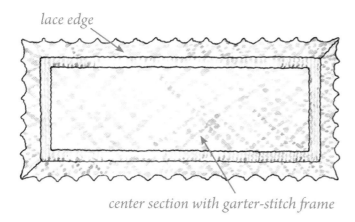

lace edge

center section with garter-stitch frame

A Haapsalu shawl is characterized by a distinct arrangement of patterns.

The shawl consists of:
• a center section with the basic stitch pattern, bordered on all sides with a garter-stitch frame;
• a separately knitted lacy edge of which the bind-off is later sewn onto the main piece.

A true Haapsalu shawl is so delicate and airy that it can pass through a ring ...

Haapsalu Scarf

A Haapsalu scarf is always square.

The length of each side is approximately 100–150 cm (40–60 in.) or 240–260 stitches.

The scarf consists of:
- a fine-patterned openwork center section and the big rich border pattern that are separated and surrounded by a garter-stitch frame
- a separately knitted lace edge of which the bind-off is later sewn onto the main piece.

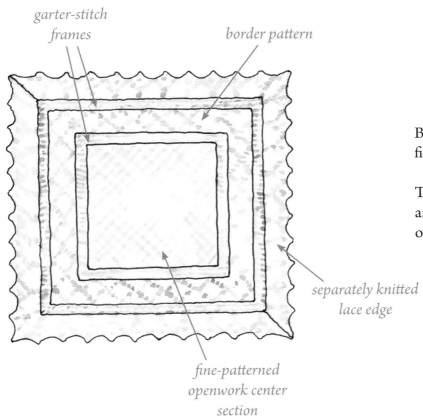

garter-stitch frames

border pattern

separately knitted lace edge

fine-patterned openwork center section

Both the shawl and the scarf are knitted of fine wool yarn in openwork lace patterns.

The patterns of Haapsalu scarves and shawls are characterized by the abundance of yarn overs and *nupps*.

How to Knit a Haapsalu Shawl

A Haapsalu shawl is always knitted in openwork lace patterns that are charted. More detailed instructions for reading the stitch patterns may be found on page 35.

A Haapsalu shawl is begun by working the center section. This center pattern determines the number of stitches for the lace edge that is later sewn onto the completed center section. The final task is blocking the shawl.

Calculate stitch count for center section

In order to calculate the suitable number of stitches to cast on, one has to bear in mind that the center section is surrounded by a garter-stitch frame where both right and wrong side rows are knitted (the first stitch of every row, the edge stitch, being slipped as to purl).

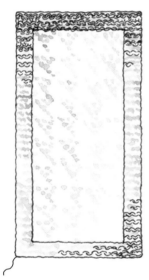

- The center section begins with three garter ridges or six knit rows.
- In addition to the center pattern, calculate four garter stitches at the beginning and end of each row.
- **Purl the wrong side rows of the pattern** if they are not shown on the chart.
- Empty squares represent stitches which do not exist.
- The shawl ends with three garter ridges.

You face the right side of the shawl when the tail from the cast-on is on your left.

Master's advice

The width of the shawl is about 115–140 stitches. The stitches are calculated as follows:
- four stitches on both sides for garter edges;
- according to the chart add stitches before and after the pattern repeat, to make the pattern mirror-image;
- repeat the pattern as many times as needed to get the desired width of the shawl.

Stitch calculation for leaf pattern with *nupps*:

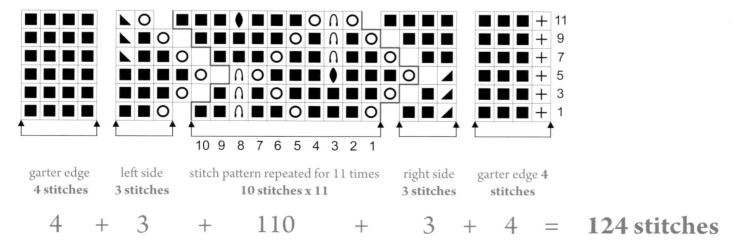

garter edge	left side	stitch pattern repeated for 11 times	right side	garter edge 4
4 stitches	**3 stitches**	**10 stitches x 11**	**3 stitches**	**stitches**

$$4 \ + \ 3 \ + \ 110 \ + \ 3 \ + \ 4 \ = \ \textbf{124 stitches}$$

Knitting the Center Section

The stitches of the center section are cast on with needles one size larger than those used for knitting the main piece (No 4–4.5 mm, US 7–8). This guarantees that the cast-on edge of the shawl stretches as much as the main piece. In order to achieve this, **the stitches are cast on by working a knitted cast-on.**

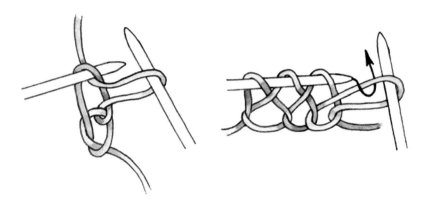

- Make a slipknot and place it onto the left-hand needle.
- Knit a stitch into the slipknot.
- Place the new stitch onto the left needle and knit into it again.

The edge of the center piece of a Haapsalu shawl **has to be loose, the edge stitches should form small loops.**

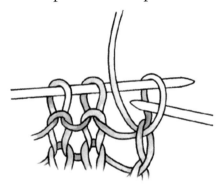

- Slip the edge stitch as to purl to the right-hand needle, so that the yarn remains in front of the needle. Place yarn to the back, between the two needles, in order to knit the next stitch.

The center section of a Haapsalu shawl is finished with a **stretchy bind-off, done on the wrong side of the piece.**

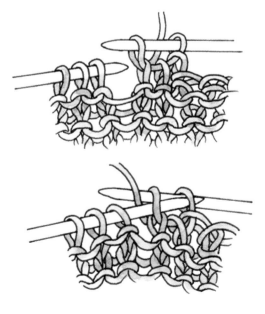

- Knit two first stitches.

- Pass them back to the left-hand needle and knit them together through the back loop (tbl).

Find stitch patterns for the center section on pages 40–179.

Lace Edge

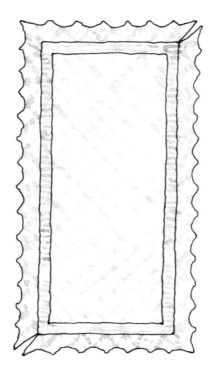

The lace edge of a Haapsalu shawl is always knitted separately, in two pieces. The bound-off edge of the completed lace edges are then attached to the center section by sewing.

The lace edge is not picked up and knitted onto the shawl, as there would then be yarn-over holes in the center of each scallop on the outer edge, which would spoil the shape of the points.

Master's explanation

The lace edge is usually worked in two pieces, and even then the number of stitches needed for the edge still remains rather large.
For knitting a lace edge, it is advisable to use either longer needles or even circular needles so the stitches fit more easily.

Calculate stitch count for lace edge

The lace edge has to be stretchy so that its outer border will form beautiful scallops when blocked. Therefore, for the lace edge you must cast on more stitches than the number of stitches across the width of the shawl and the garter ridges on both sides. More stitches are also added for each corner where the straight lace edge has to curve, creating handsome scallops.

To calculate the stitch count for the lace edge you need to know:

- *The number of stitches of the center piece (henceforth: shawl stitches)*
- *The number of garter ridges along the length of the shawl. For this, count either the garter ridges or edge stitches along the length of the center piece – there is one edge stitch for every two garter rows or for every one garter ridge (henceforth: edge stitches)*

Placement of extra stitches at the corners and along the length of the shawl.

The number of stitches shown on the chart corresponds to every shawl stitch (or edge stitch).

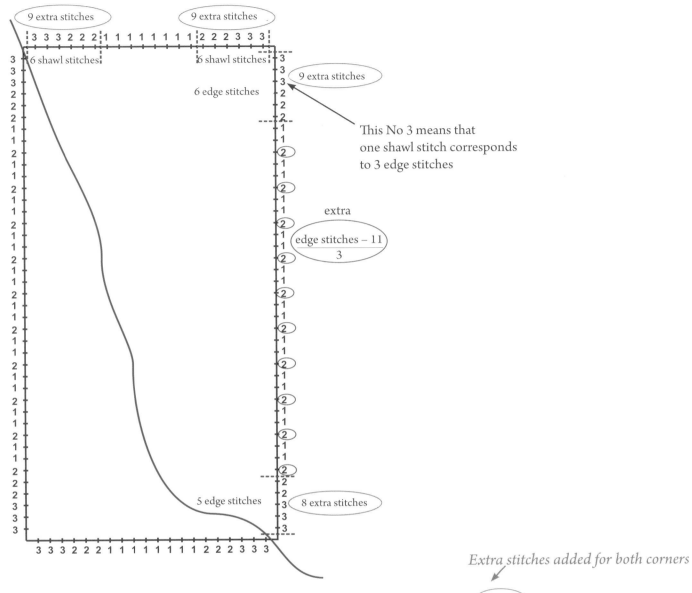

1. Number of edge stitches in the width of the shawl = shawl stitches + 9 + 9 = **shawl stitches + 18 stitches**

2. Number of edge stitches on one side (length) of the shawl =

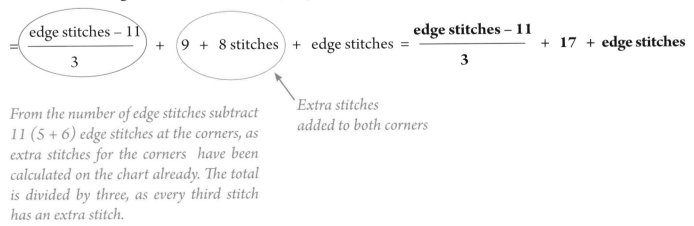

$$= \left(\frac{\text{edge stitches} - 11}{3} \right) + \left(9 + 8 \text{ stitches} \right) + \text{edge stitches} = \frac{\textbf{edge stitches} - 11}{3} + \textbf{17} + \textbf{edge stitches}$$

From the number of edge stitches subtract 11 (5 + 6) edge stitches at the corners, as extra stitches for the corners have been calculated on the chart already. The total is divided by three, as every third stitch has an extra stitch.

Extra stitches added to both corners

Add both numbers to get the grand total of stitches for the lace edging.

For example:

the center piece of the shawl has 124 stitches (shawl stitches)
one side of the shawl has 220 garter ridges (edge stitches)

Stitch count for lace edge:

for the width = 124 stitches + 18 stitches = **142** stitches

$$\textbf{for the lenght} = \frac{220 - 11}{3} + 17 \text{ stitches} + 220 = 69.6 + 17 + 220 = \textbf{306.6} \text{ stitches}$$

TOTAL 142 + 306.6 = 448.6 stitches ≈ **449** stitches

To avoid half-finished scallops on the lace edge, the number of stitches needs to correspond with the stitch pattern.
Therefore, add as many stitches as are necessary to get full repeats of the lace pattern.

Lace Edge pattern

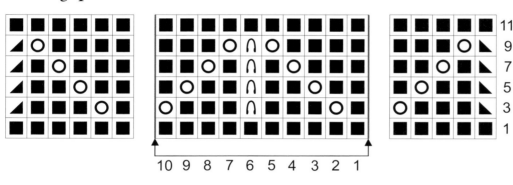

left-side edge pattern	pattern repeat	right-side edge pattern
6 stitches	**number of stitches divisible by 10**	**5 stitches**

According to the formula, 449 stitches have been calculated for the lace edge.
To find the number of stitches you need (adjusting for the number in the pattern repeat) to subtract the number of edge pattern stitches (stitches at the right and left sides of the main repeat) from the total number of stitches calculated in the formula (449 – 5 – 6 = 438 stitches).
The result has to be rounded up to obtain a number that would equal the number of stitches in a 10-stitch lace repeat (the closest number divisible by 10 is 440).
To the resulting number add the number of stitches at the right and left sides of the main repeat again (440 + 5 + 6 = **451**).

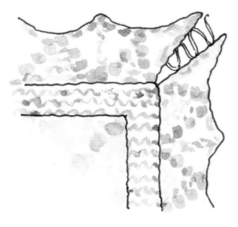

The lace edge patterns of Haapsalu shawls are charted so that the lace edge begins and ends with the center of a scallop. In this way, the two separately worked lace pieces will meet and beautiful points will be formed at each corner of the shawl after sewing.

Knitting the Lace Edge

The stitches of the lace edge of a Haapsalu shawl are cast on by working a knitted cast-on (see page 27). **The cast-on is worked with the yarn doubled** to add weight and strength to the cast-on edge.

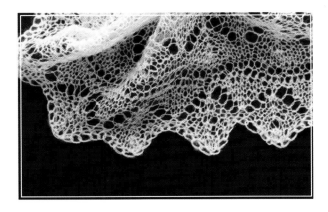

The cast-on of the lace edge makes up the outer, scalloped edge of the shawl which will, thanks to the doubled yarn in casting on, be clearly visible, in high relief.

- The stitches of the lace edge are cast on by using needles one or two sizes larger than those used for the body of the shawl. This helps to achieve a stretchy edge and beautifully formed scallops.

When casting on, mark every 50th or 100th stitch with a small piece of yarn. This will make it easier to count stitches and later, in working the pattern, avoid mistakes in the first row of the pattern.

- Continue to work the lace edge with a single strand and in garter stitch, i.e. both right side and wrong side rows are knitted. By doing this, the edge of the shawl will not curl.

Work the whole lace edge with needles one size larger than the shawl, so that when blocking, the lace edge will stretch as much as the center section.

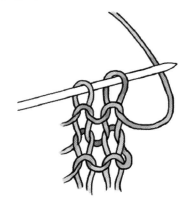

- The outer edge stitches of the lace edging are formed into small knots, the first stitch is not slipped, but rather, it is knit. In order to obtain this knotted edge, take the yarn around the outer edge, to the back, when knitting the first stitch.

- The lace edge of a Haapsalu shawl is bound off on the wrong side row using a stretchy knitted bind-off (see page 27).

See lace edge patterns on pages 180–182.

Join lace edge to center section

The lace edge is sewn onto the center section **on the wrong side** of the shawl and the lace edge, so the right sides of each piece are facing each other.

The wrong side of the lace edge can be recognized by its cast on border.

 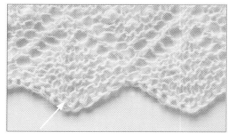

On the wrong side you can see the complete cast on chain, made of two strands of yarn, on the edge.

On the right side only one side of the cast on chain, made of two strands of yarn, shows on the edge.

Master's advice

- Before sewing, distribute the lace edge onto the shawl by counting the scallops. For this you need to calculate the lace edge stitches meant for the width and length of the shawl (see calculate stitch count for lace edge on page 29). Each corner of the shawl should meet at the exact center of a scallop on the lace edge.

  Keeping in mind the extra stitches, secure the lace edge from the corners and central parts to the shawl with the help of pins. By doing this, you can avoid an unpleasant surprise at the opposite corner of the shawl, discovering that the length of the lace edge is insufficient or too long.

- Start sewing at one corner of the center section from the right to the left. By following the diagram, bring the threaded needle through each loop of the edge of both pieces without skipping any loops. Take only one loop from the center piece and, according to the diagram, one, two or three loops from the cast-off of the lace edge. Bring the needle through a single thread of the loop towards the seam.

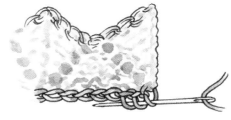

- Join the lace edge onto the center piece without cutting the yarn.

Master's advice

Thread a blunt point needle with the yarn attached to the ball and sew the whole lace edge to the center at one time, with this yarn, carefully pulling on the sewing yarn every now and then. When stretched, the seam should be as elastic as the knitted center piece and the lace edge.

The diagram of joining the lace edge to center section

- When sewing, bring the threaded needle through only one loop of the center section, whereas the loops of the lace edge are taken up according to the following diagram.

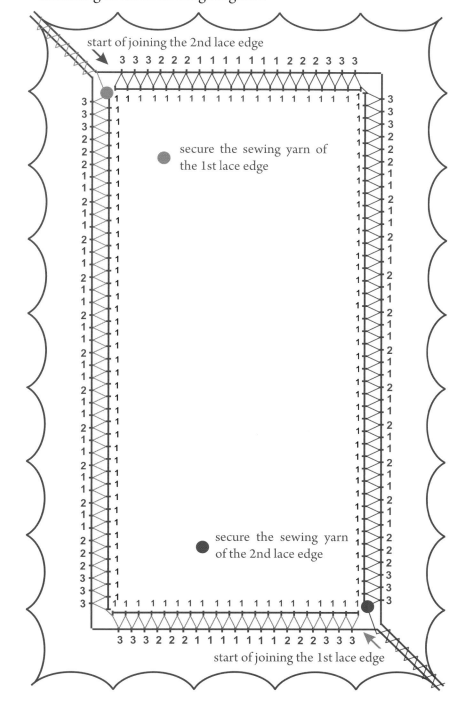

The extra stitches, added to the cast-on of the edge to get full repeats of the lace pattern as well as errors in sewing, can best be hidden by making small adjustments in the diagram in the middle of the longer sides of the shawl.

- After having finished joining the lace edge and before weaving in the sewing yarn, stretch the seam so that it will not break during blocking.

- Secure both yarn tails with some stitches on the corners of the center section and do not weave them in or cut them yet.

- Join the second lace edge to the other side of the shawl in the same manner.

- Sew the ends of the lace edge together at the corners, using the yarn tails that were not woven in earlier.

Finishing

The yarn tails left over after sewing are woven in, either in the cast on edge of the lace edge or into the seams.

The completed shawl is hand washed gently with a mild soap and warm water. Squeeze gently, never felt or wring!

The Haapsalu shawl becomes really beautiful only after blocking. For this, the washed and still wet shawl is mounted onto the frame pinning out each point of the lace edge. During blocking be sure that the pattern is straight.

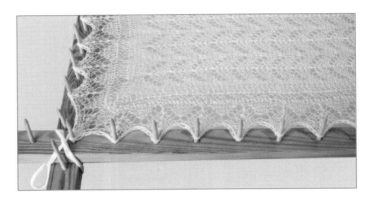

Allow the shawl to air-dry on the frame.

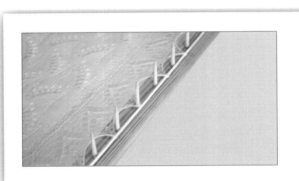

Master's advice

If the pegs of the frame do not correspond to the scallops on the lace edge, stick a rod or long double pointed knitting needle through the point of each scallop and place the rod behind the pegs of the frame.

After drying pick up each cast-on stitch (made of doubled yarn) of the lace edge onto a knitting needle and stretch the edge a little so that it will become more open and that a perfect looped edge may be formed.

Master's advice

Pick up each doubled outer edge stitch on the lace edge onto three or four needles, wet the stitches a little and leave to dry. After drying remove the needles and tidy up each point separately by pulling it from the tip and between the scallops.

Finally fold the Haapsalu shawl so that the points of the lace edge line up with opposite points and leave it under a weight (for example, a pillow) for at least one day. This way, the shape of the shawl is maintained.

Reading of stitch patterns

In Estonia, stitch patterns are charted. In order to read these charts one has to know the symbols which represent corresponding stitches (see stitch guide on pages 36-37). A stitch pattern presented in this way is clearly arranged and easy to follow.

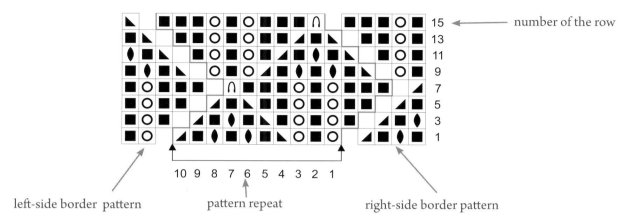

left-side border pattern — pattern repeat — right-side border pattern

- Read the chart starting from the right side of the bottom row. All the right side rows are marked with numbers.
- All the symbols on the charts indicate what you should actually do on the row, not what the row looks like from the front of the work.
- The right side row is always started at the side of the chart with the number.
- In most of the lace patterns from Haapsalu, only uneven-numbered rows (1, 3, 5, etc) are charted. In this case, all even-numbered rows or **wrong side rows** (2, 4, 6, etc), when they do not show on the chart, are purled.
- If even–numbered or wrong side rows are shown on the chart, begin reading the row from the side with the number, i.e. from the left. The symbols on this row indicate what you should actually do with the stitch, if the symbol is a knit, you should knit the stitch, if it is the symbol for purl, then purl it, etc.

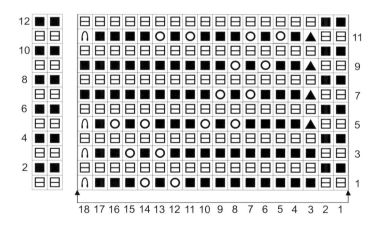

Arrows and red lines are used in the chart to separate the pattern repeat – part of the pattern that is repeated, if necessary.

- The stitches of a pattern repeat are numbered. This facilitates calculating the number of stitches needed for the knitted item.
- If the stitch pattern includes border patterns (parts of the pattern that allows the two sides to mirror each other or otherwise make a good transition at the right and left sides of the pattern), the latter are separated from the pattern repeat by empty squares that have to be ignored during knitting – these stitches do not exist. The empty space facilitates reading the pattern repeat.
- If the pattern repeat has border patterns, one needs to work the right-side border pattern first, then repeat the pattern for the desired number of times and finally work the left-side border pattern.

Stitch Guide

+ Edge stitch
Slip the first stitch to the right-hand needle as to purl.

■ Knit stitch (k)

⊟ Purl stitch (p)

◆ Twisted knit stitch or Knit one stitch through the back loop (k1tbl)
Insert right-hand needle into back loop of stitch on left-hand needle from right to left and knit.

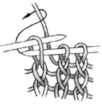

○ Yarn over (yo)
Bring yarn to front between the two needles, then bring yarn over right-hand needle from front to back.

◤ Knit two stitches together (k2tog)

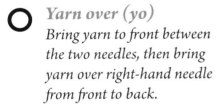

◣ Slip one, knit one, pass the slipped stitch over (sl 1, k1, psso)
Slip first stitch as to knit, knit next stitch, then pass slipped stitch over.

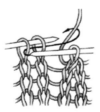

◿ Purl two stitches together (p2tog)

▲ Knit three stitches together (k3tog)

◭ Purl three stitches together (p3tog)

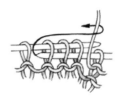

∩ Slip one, knit two together, pass slipped stitch over (sl 1, k2tog, psso)
Slip first stitch as to knit, knit two together, pass slipped stitch over.

⋀ Three stitches together centered (sl 2 as if to knit, k1, p2sso)
Slip two stitches as to knit at the same time, knit next stitch and pass two slipped stitches over knitted stitch

⨯ 2 / 2 — 2 Gathered stitches or 2 stitches from 2
Knit two together, leave original two stitches on left-hand needle, knit into back loops of these two stitches again.

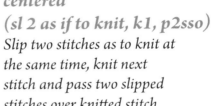

⨯ 3/3 5/5 — 3 or 5 Gathered stitches or 3 (5) stitches from 3 (5)
Knit three (five) together, do not remove original stitches from left-hand needle, yarn over, knit original three (five) together again. For five stitches, yarn over and knit original five stitches together one more time.

36

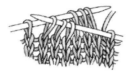

Cable to the right

Slip three stitches onto cable needle and hold in back of work, knit three stitches, then knit three stitches from cable needle.

Cable to the left

Slip three knit stitches onto cable needle and hold in front of work, knit three stitches, then knit three stitches from cable needle.

Nupp (button or bobble)

*Knit into stitch, leaving it on the left-hand needle, * yarn over, knit into original stitch again, repeat from * two more times – seven stitches from one stitch.*

If nupp is increased on right side row then purl all nupp stitches together on wrong side row.

If nupp is increased on wrong side row then knit the nupp stitches together through the back loops on right side row.

Master's advice

In order to get a beautiful *nupp* stretch the loops of the *nupps* so that they are even and long enough. This makes it easier to purl or knit them together on the following row.

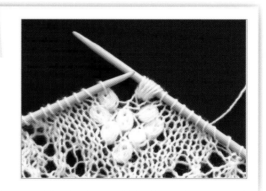

*F*or me the Haapsalu shawl is like Haapsalu itself – beautiful, small in size, pleasantly old-fashioned and sweetly bourgeois.

Karin Rask, actress

The scarf with the Silvia pattern was knitted by Miralda Piper.

Stitch Patterns

During the early years of knitting Haapsalu scarves and shawls the patterns were shared, from hand to hand, from mothers to daughters, from one neighbor to another. The knitters did not use graphed symbols at that time, they knew the patterns by heart or used completed shawls as examples. Unraveling an old shawl was also a method for learning the pattern. Ideas for new patterns were derived mostly from nature and everyday life. This early period gave birth to the leaf (*lehekiri*), money (*rahakiri*) and twig (*hagakiri*) patterns.

Later on, shawl knitters started to collect stitch patterns on long and narrow, knitted samplers. One knitter could have several samplers of this kind. These were also lent to neighbors for learning new stitch patterns. Traditionally the loan was repaid with a new pattern added to the sampler. However, there were patterns that were kept as family secrets and were handed down only from mother to daughter.

ERM A 592: 92. Sampler of Haapsalu patterns from 1926. This 162 cm long strip contains 40 lacy patterns. It was given to the museum by lace knitter Marie Arujõe (born in 1901).

Printed patterns with graphed symbols came into use in the 1930s. The first known knitter to graph stitch patterns was the handicraft teacher at Haapsalu 1st Primary School, Matilde Möll (1880–1942). According to other data it was her mother, Julie Valdmann, who started using graphed symbols.

In 1967, all the lace knitters of UKU craft cooperative had to knit samplers. Together with charts and written instructions, the samplers were sent to Tallinn and assembled by UKU into a pattern album from which patterns were then distributed all over Estonia.

In the course of time, different groups of shawl patterns have developed. Each group is based on a historical pattern from which many different new variations have been derived. For example, there are lily of the valley patterns (*piibelehekiri*), leaf patterns (*lehekiri*) and head of grain patterns (*viljapeakiri*).

A separate group is made up of patterns that are connected with shawls and scarves given to celebrated persons as gifts (celebrities' patterns).

The patterns in this book have been collected from the present lace knitters of Haapsalu – Linda Elgas, Maiva Dunkel, Saima Tee, Helga Rüütel, Aime Edasi, Laine Põldme, Helmi Mändla, Viivi Palmiste, Miralda Piper, Aasa Jõelaid, Mall Kütt, Malle Yeremeyeva and Aime Saareleht. They kindly allowed the authors to use their patterns that have been assembled, changed and improved on over many years. There are also early patterns created by unknown knitters.

Samplers that reveal the real beauty of patterns were knitted for this book by:

Linda Elgas,	*Malle Yeremeyeva,*
Maiva Dunkel,	*Siiri Reimann,*
Saima Tee,	*Elgi Simulask,*
Helga Rüütel,	*Tiia Kaus,*
Aime Edasi,	*Ruth Bormann,*
Laine Põldme,	*Mirje Sims,*
Silvi Saarlo,	*Elfride Ohtla,*
Helmi Mändla,	*Marta Kumari,*
Viivi Palmiste,	*Aive Ploom,*
Miralda Piper,	*Ly Härm,*
Mall Kütt,	*Aime Saareleht.*

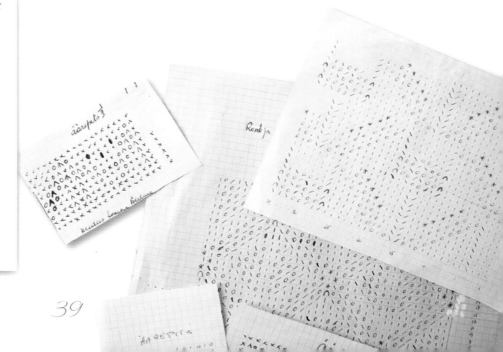

(VI SUMFOONIAST)

Tchaikovsky's Bench in Haapsalu. The shawl was knitted by Helga Rüütel.

Crown Prince Pattern

In the summer of 1932 the Swedish Crown Prince and future King Gustav VI Adolf paid a visit to Estonia in connection with the 300th jubilee of the University of Tartu. He also stopped in the „capital" of Estonian Swedes, Haapsalu. As a souvenir, a Haapsalu scarf was presented to the Crown Prince by Mayor Hans Alver. The scarf was knitted by Julie Valdmann. The pattern was designed by her daughter, Matilde Möll, handicraft teacher at Haapsalu Primary School. As the scarf given to the eminent guest had to be something special, she used ancient mitten patterns in the design. This was a completely new approach since, until this time, nature had been the only source of inspiration for scarf patterns (for example: leaf patterns, butterfly patterns).

Layout of patterns on the shawl (stitch patterns of the motifs on the next page)

Crown Prince Shawl, Motif 1

Kroonprintsi salli motiiv 1

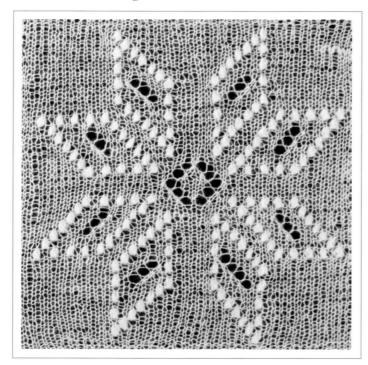

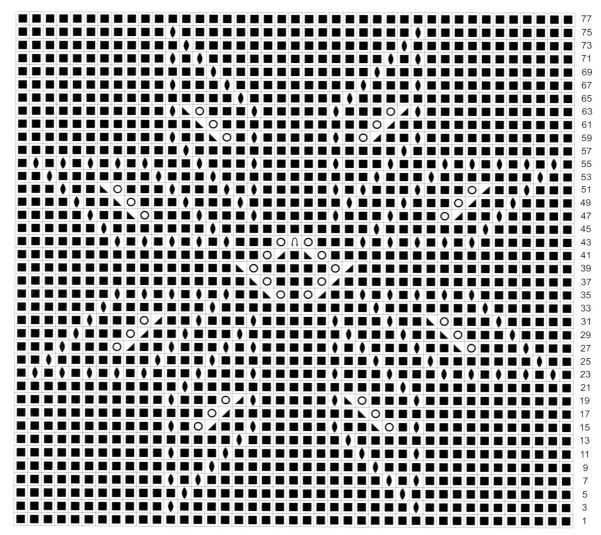

Crown Prince Shawl, Motif 2

Kroonprintsi salli motiiv 2

Sundial in Haapsalu.
The shawl was knitted by
Viivi Palmiste.

Greta Garbo Pattern

In 1936, a big commercial fair was held in New York, where Estonia was represented by Haapsalu scarves. This offered a good opportunity to fulfill the dream of Haapsalu knitters – to give a stylish scarf to the legendary film star, Greta Garbo. With the help from the consul general of the Republic of Estonia, Karl Kuusik, a scarf with heart motifs was presented to the actress, then living in the USA. The pattern design, comprised of hearts, was thereafter named after Greta Garbo. Both the scarves displayed in the exhibition and this gift brought recognition to Haapsalu scarves from all over the world. Alas, there is no evidence whether the secret hope of the knitters, that the „divine Greta" would wear the scarf in one of her movies, ever came true.

Greta Garbo Pattern 1

Greta Garbo kiri 1

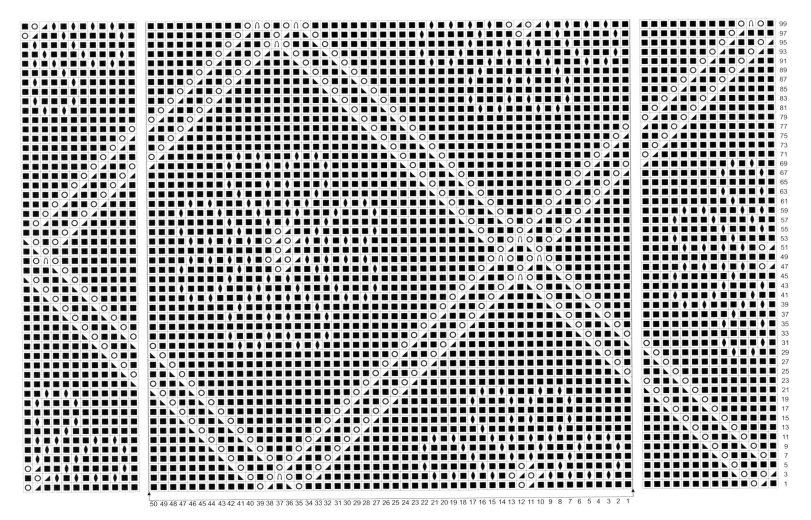

Haapsalu railway station.
The shawl was knitted
by Miralda Piper.

Greta Garbo
Pattern

The Greta Garbo pattern, beloved by many knitters, has been improved a little in the course of time. As well as the original design there are several different Greta Garbo patterns that are used today.

Greta Garbo Pattern 2
Greta Garbo kiri 2

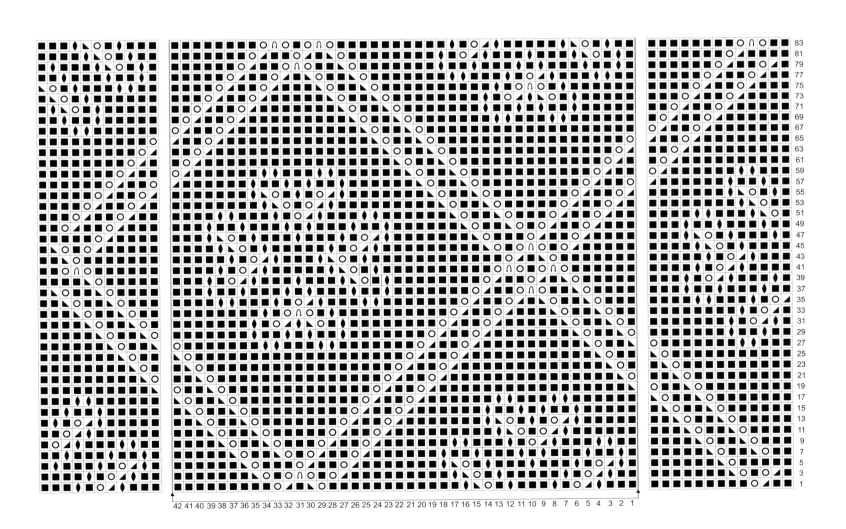

*Haapsalu Episcopal Castle.
This shawl was knitted
by Aasa Jõelaid.*

Presenting the shawl to Queen Silvia.

Silvia Pattern

In the spring of 1992 Haapsalu was visited by Swedish King Carl XVI Gustav and Queen Silvia. The Haapsalu shawl, with a special design of a lily of the valley pattern, was considered the most suitable gift for the stately guests. The shawl was knitted by Helga Puusepp.

The design of this shawl comes from the late 1970s when UKU master knitters were updating their production and the lily of the valley pattern was improved in every possible way. The most beautiful variation (author A. Jõelaid, art. 3932) was chosen for the shawl to be given to the Queen. Today this design is known as Silvia pattern; different variations of it make up the most popular patterns of the Haapsalu shawl repertoire.

Silvia Pattern
Silvia kiri

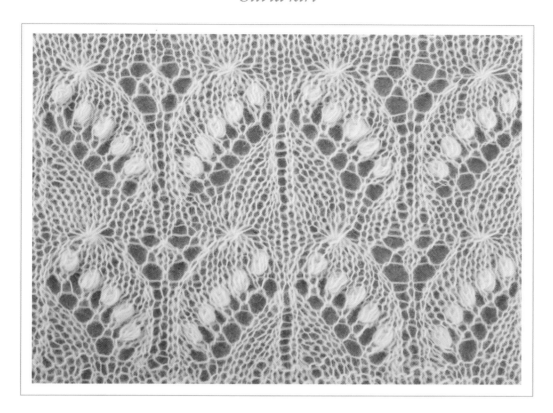

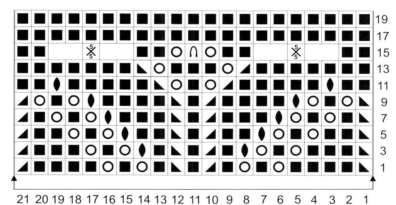

The Silvia pattern is considered to be nice by many. No wonder that when the opportunity came to give a lace shawl to Helle Meri, wife of Lennart Meri, the first President of the Republic of Estonia (having regained its independence), the master knitters made their decision in favor of this shawl design.

The shawl was presented to Mrs Helle Meri by the head of the Haapsalu Handicraft Society, Silvi Saarlo, on 29 June, 1999 at the reception of the presidential couple in Kadriorg Palace in Tallinn.

Silvia Pattern 2
Silvia kiri 2

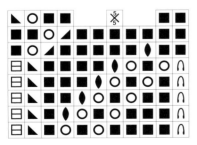

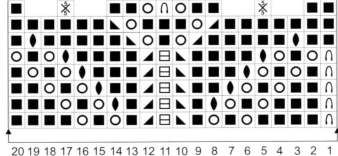

20 19 18 17 16 15 14 13 12 11 10 9 8 7 6 5 4 3 2 1

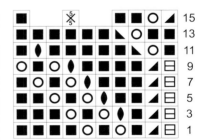

Silvia Pattern 3
Silvia kiri 3

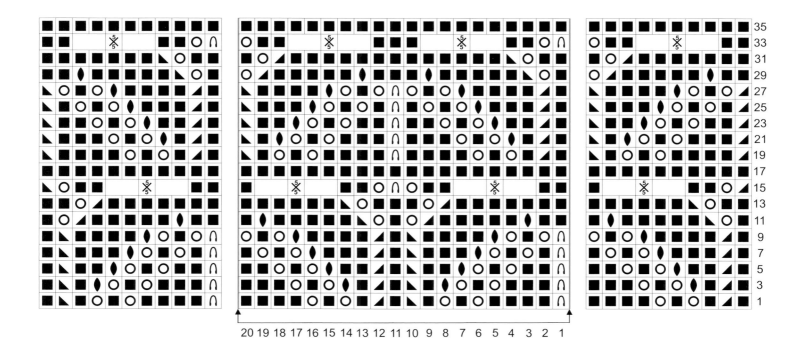

This shawl was knitted by Helmi Mändla.

Presenting the shawl to Mrs Rüütel in the handicraft shop

Ingrid Rüütel Pattern

In August 2003 Läänemaa County was visited by the then presidential couple, Arnold and Ingrid Rüütel. During the visit Mrs Ingrid Rüütel visited the Ehte Handicraft and Art Shop in Haapsalu.

The master knitters gave the First Lady a shawl done in a lily of the valley with leaf pattern, made by Miralda Piper. The UKU chronicle ascribes the design to Ester Viilup. Today this lily of the valley with leaf pattern is known as the Ingrid Rüütel pattern.

Ingrid Rüütel Pattern

Ingrid Rüütli kiri

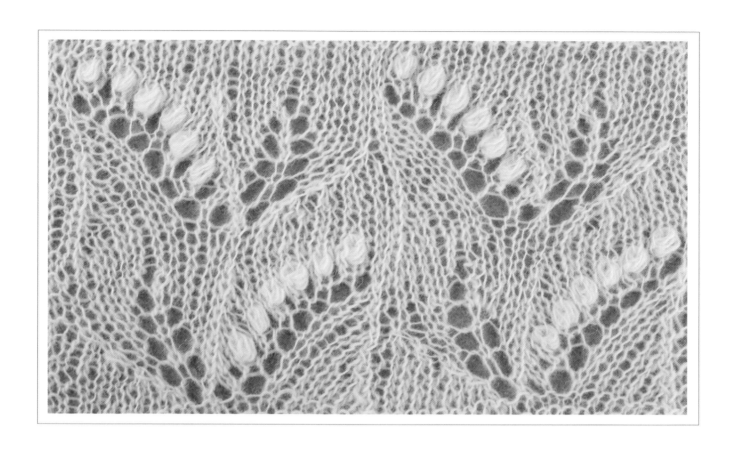

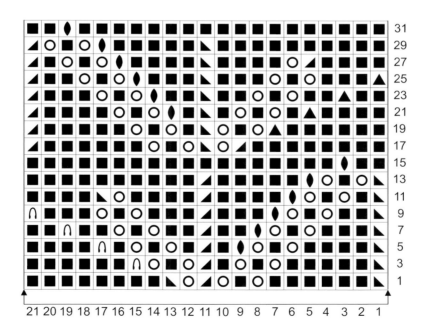

The shawl was knitted by Helmi Mändla.

Mrs Evelin Ilves Shawl

When Toomas Hendrik Ilves was elected the new President of Estonia in 2006, the women of Haapsalu Handicraft Society started to discuss right away which pattern should be used in a shawl for Evelin Ilves. The most suitable shawl for the young First Lady was considered to be of a flowered design. The shawl was completed by Helmi Mändla. When the presidential couple visited Läänemaa County in 2008, the flowered shawl was presented to Mrs Evelin in the Müüriääre Cafe in Haapsalu.

Evelin Ilves Pattern

Evelin Ilvese kiri

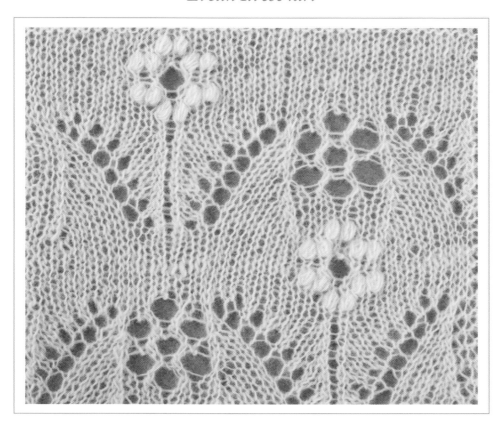

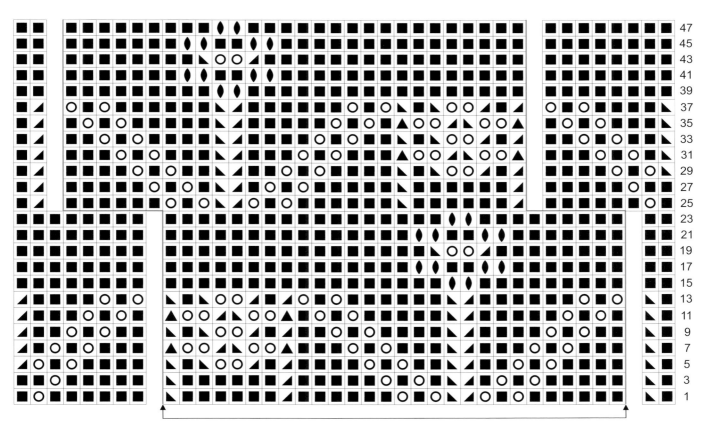

Haapsalu Episcopal Castle. The shawl was knitted by Aime Edasi.

Queen Sofia Shawl

On 4 May, 2009 the Spanish King Juan Carlos I and Queen Sofia arrived on their first state visit to Estonia. The President's Office placed an order to the master knitters for a gift to be given to the Queen – a Haapsalu shawl the pattern of which would not be recognized. A less-known design was found from the UKU chronicles; shawls with this pattern were knitted in the 1970s by Sinaida Sõer (1916–1980). The shawl for the Spanish Queen was completed by Aime Edasi.

Sofia Pattern

Sofia kiri

We all come from our childhood, and the delicate patterns of home accompany us throughout our lives!

Elle Kull, actress

The shawl was knitted by Aime Edasi.

Lily of the Valley Patterns

Lily of the valley patterns are also known as May Lily patterns. This is one of the largest groups of stitch patterns known for these shawls. They are popular among the knitters and wearers of the shawls due to the abundance of *nupps*. These numerous stitch patterns have all been derived from the simple lily of the valley pattern.

Reversed Lily of the Valley Pattern
Pööratud piibelehekiri

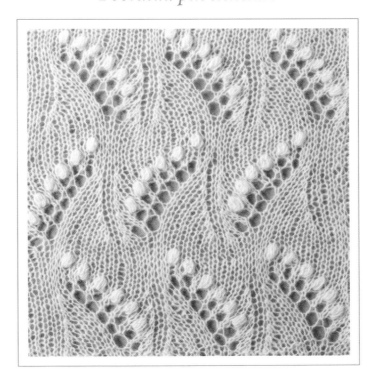

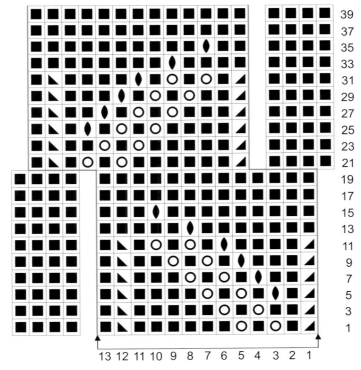

Lily of the Valley Pattern
Piibelehekiri

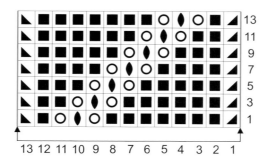

Blossomless Lily of the Valley Pattern
Õiteta piibelehekiri

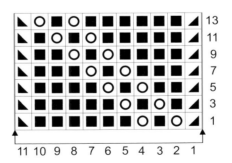

Wild Lily of the Valley Pattern

Metspiibelehekiri

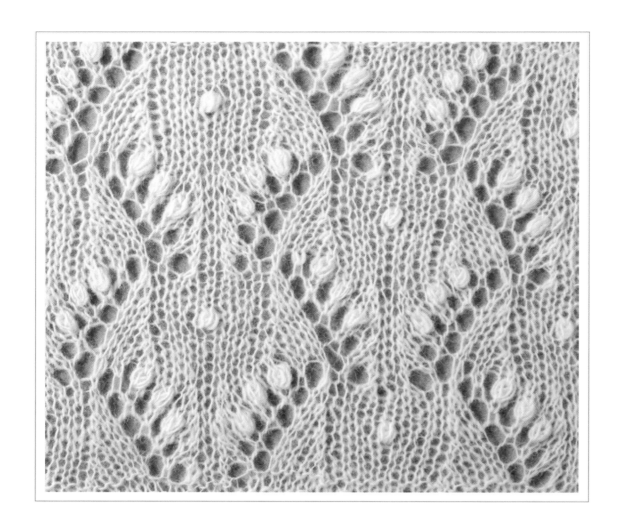

Lily of the Valley Pattern on a Leaf Motif

Piibelehekiri lehel

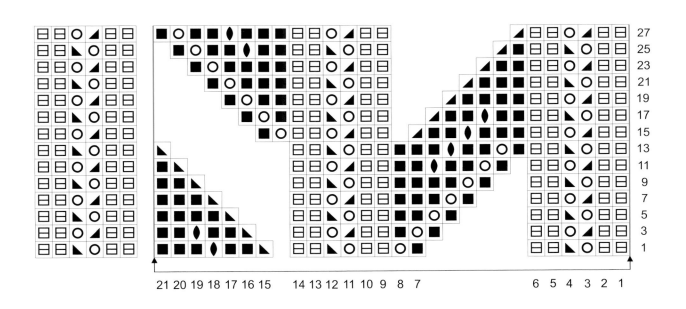

Lily of the Valley and Stones Pattern
Kividega piibelehekiri

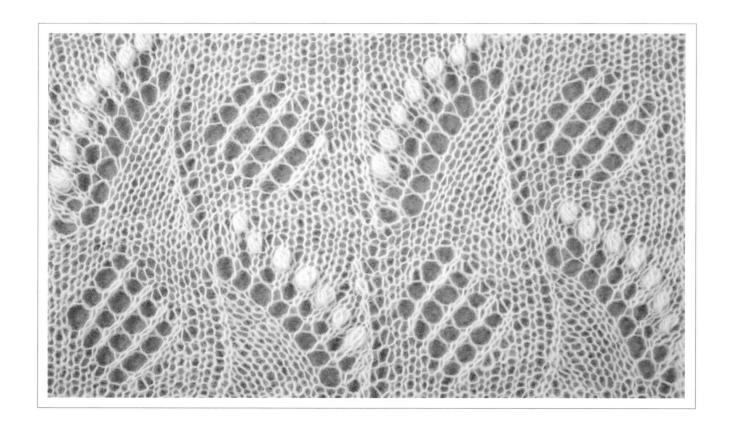

If even–numbered or wrong side rows are shown on the chart, begin reading the row from the side with the number, i.e. from the left. The symbols on this row indicate what you should actually do with the stitch, if the symbol is a knit, you should knit the stitch, if it is the symbol for purl, then purl it, etc.

Lily of the Valley and Flower Pattern 1

Lillega piibelehekiri 1

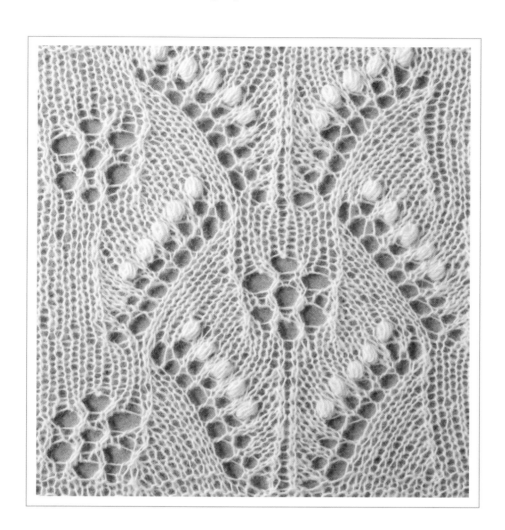

Lily of the Valley and Flower Pattern 2

Lillega piibelehekiri 2

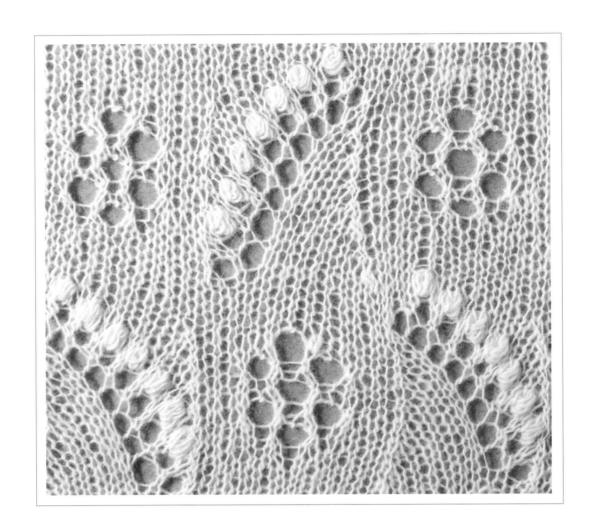

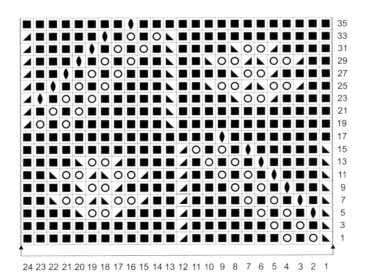

Lily of the Valley and Flower Pattern 3
Lillega piibelehekiri 3

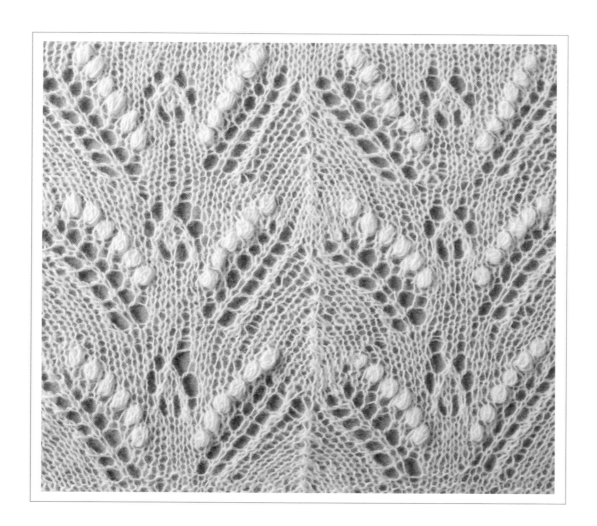

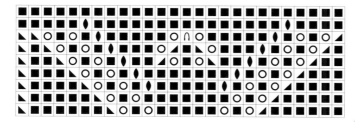

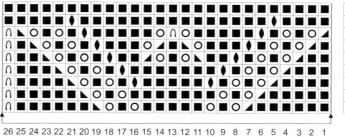

Lily of the Valley and Flower Pattern 4
Lillega piibelehekiri 4

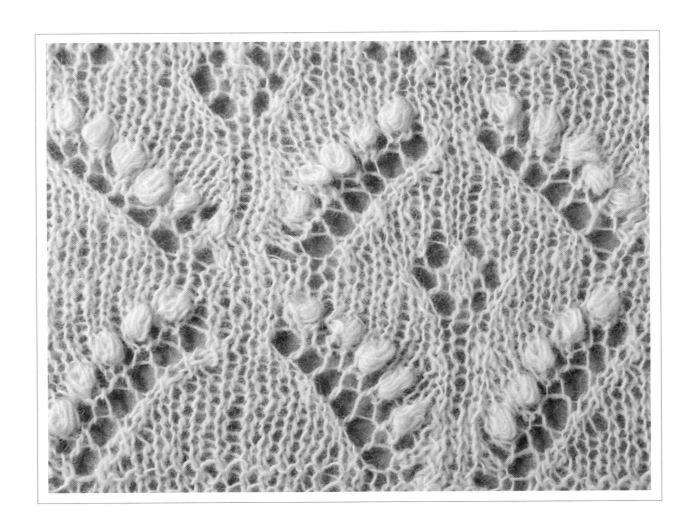

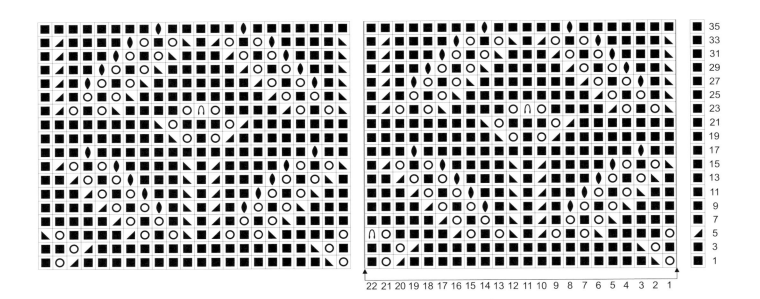

Lily of the Valley and Flower Pattern 5
Lillega piibelehekiri 5

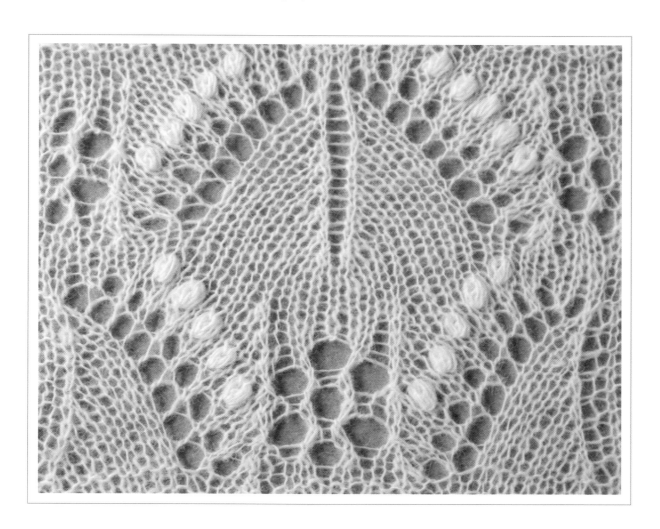

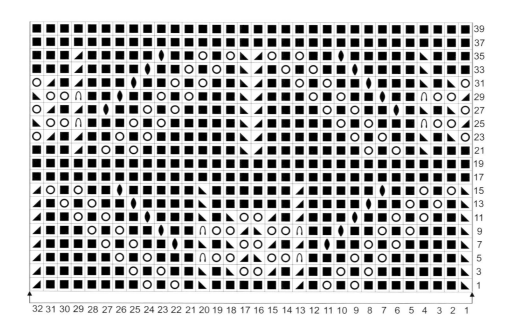

Lily of the Valley with Tulip Pattern

Tulbiga piibelehekiri

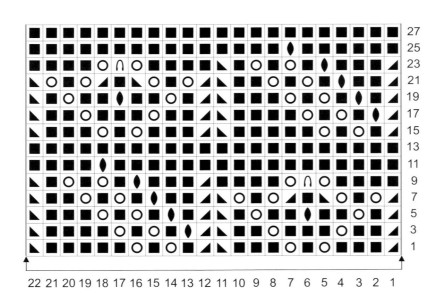

Pseudo Lily of the Valley and Flower Pattern

Lillega ebapiibelehekiri

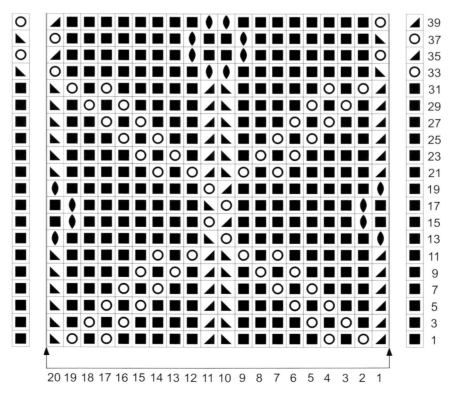

I had such a good childhood at grandma's and grandpa's in Haapsalu.

Ilon Wikland, artist and book illustrator

MINU VANAEMA MAJA
IN MY GRANDMOTHER'S HOUSE

The shawl was knitted by Aime Edasi

Double Lily of the Valley Pattern

Topeltpiibelehekiri

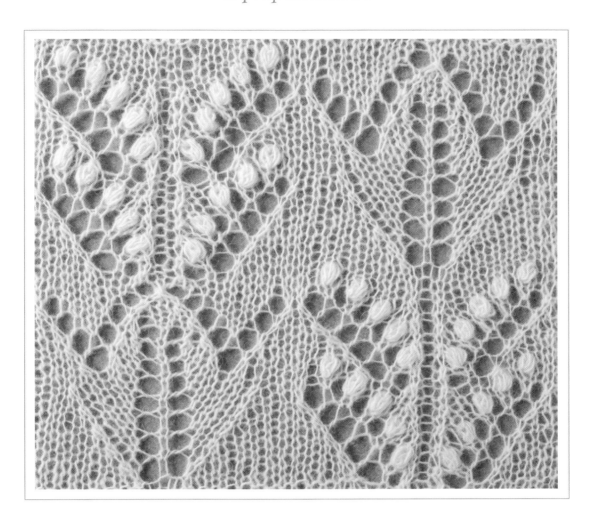

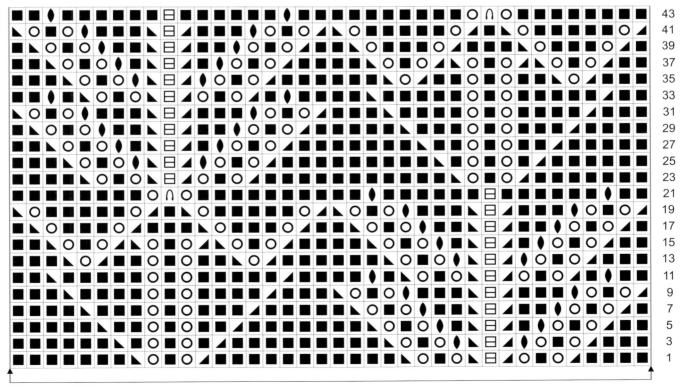

38 37 36 35 34 33 32 31 30 29 28 27 26 25 24 23 22 21 20 19 18 17 16 15 14 13 12 11 10 9 8 7 6 5 4 3 2 1

Lily of the Valley and Spruce Pattern
Kuusega piibelehekiri

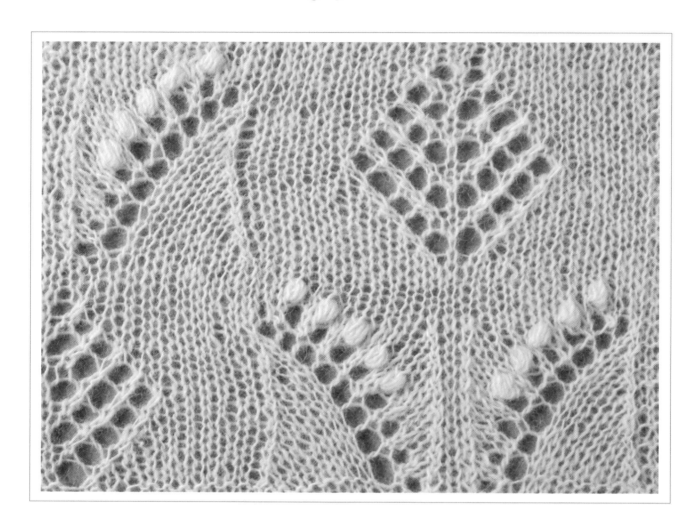

Lily of the Valley Pattern
Piibelehekiri

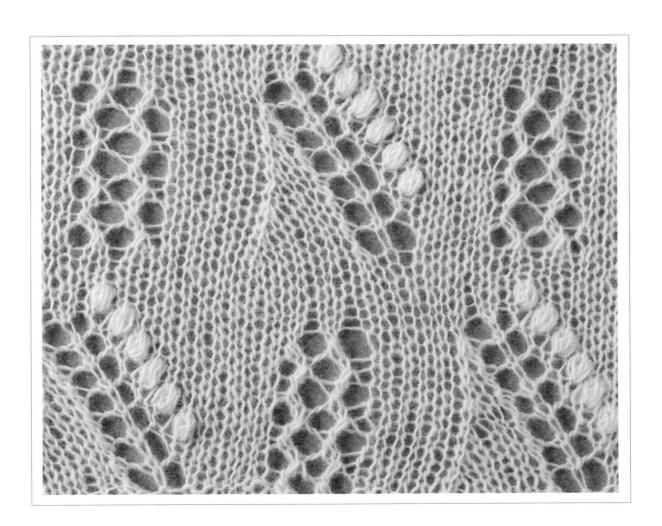

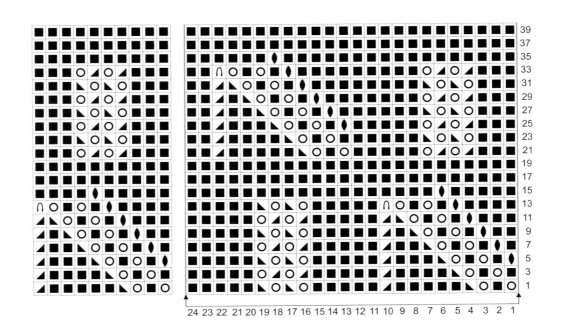

The Haapsalu shawl reminds me of a silver thread from the dreams in a fairy tale – it is fragile, beautiful and mighty, – and it protects you from the evil eye!

Epp Maria Kokamägi, painter

The poncho was knit by Aime Edasi

Pasqueflower Patterns

Pasqueflower patterns are derived from lily of the valley patterns and are characterized by the curly texture that was added to the design. Nevertheless, many masters still refer to pasqueflower patterns as lily of the valley patterns.

Pasqueflower Pattern 1
Karukellakiri 1

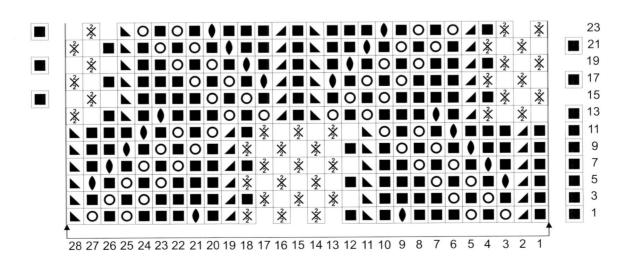

Pasqueflower Pattern 2
Karukellakiri 2

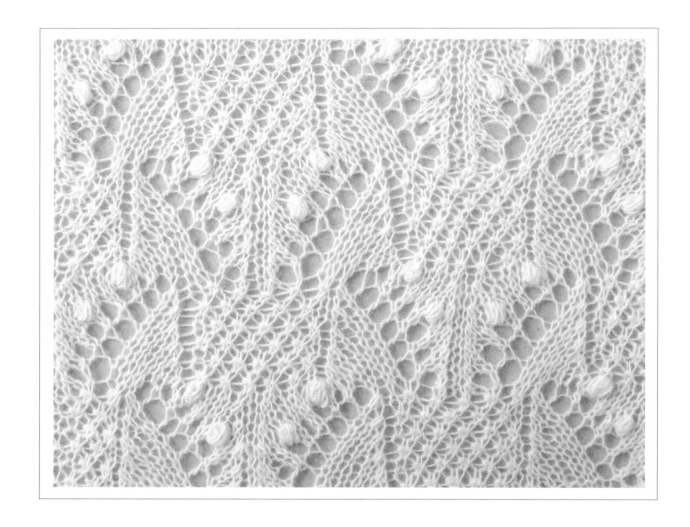

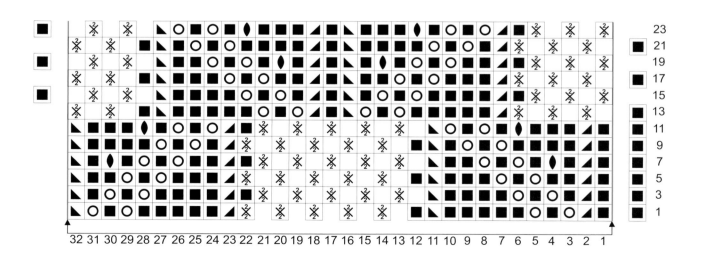

Pasqueflower Pattern 3
Karukellakiri 3

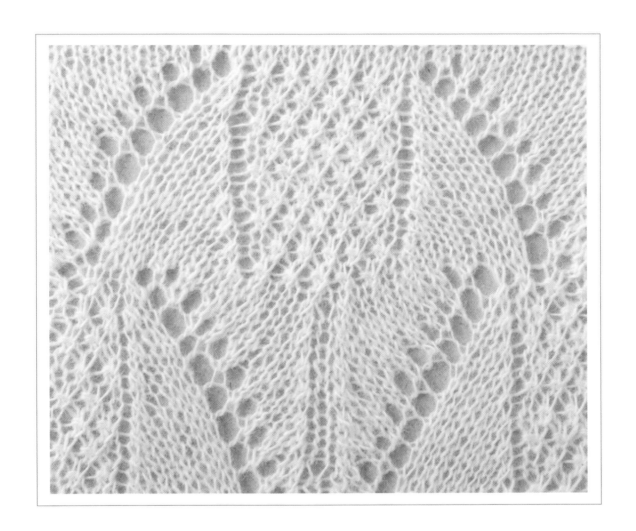

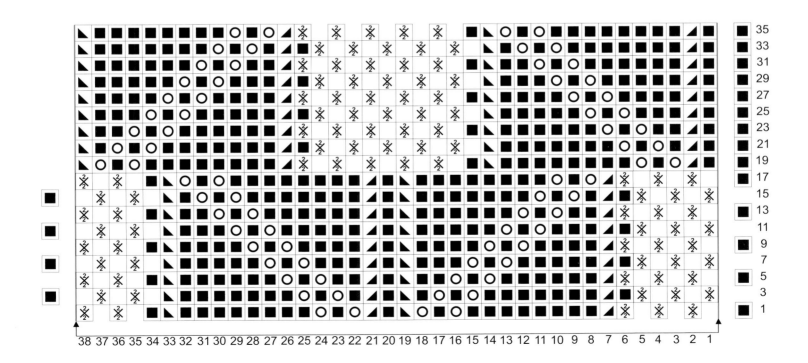

Pasqueflower Pattern 4
Karukellakiri 4

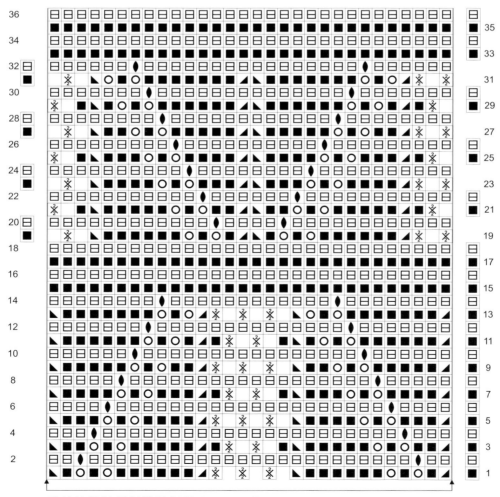

If even–numbered or wrong side rows are shown on the chart, begin reading the row from the side with the number, i.e. from the left. The symbols on this row indicate what you should actually do with the stitch, if the symbol is a knit, you should knit the stitch, if it is the symbol for purl, then purl it, etc.

Pasqueflower Pattern 5

Karukellakiri 5

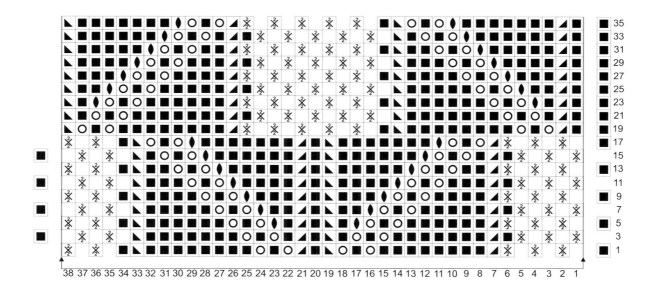

The shawl was knitted by Elgi Simulask

Leaf Patterns

One of the oldest groups of stitch patterns is made up of leaf shapes that were designed in the 19th century. The masters of that time favored motifs inspired by the surrounding nature. As our nature has been a generous source of inspiration, the number of leaf patterns accumulated during all these years is extensive.

Lilac Leaf Pattern 1
Sirelilehekiri 1

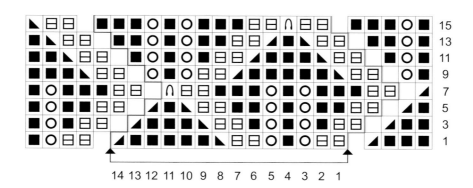

Lilac Leaf Pattern 2
Sirelilehekiri 2

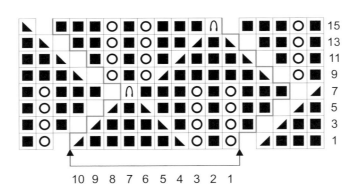

Lilac Leaf Pattern 3

Sirelilehekiri 3

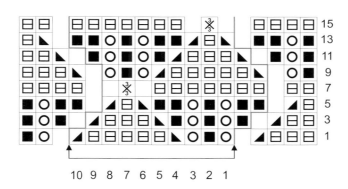

Lilac Leaf Pattern with Nupps
Nuppudega sirelilehekiri

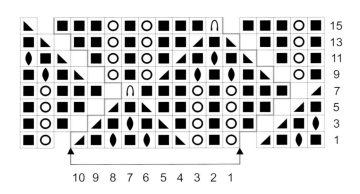

Leaf Pattern 1
Lehekiri 1

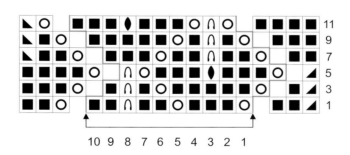

This leaf pattern can also be made without nupps.

Leaf Pattern 2
Lehekiri 2

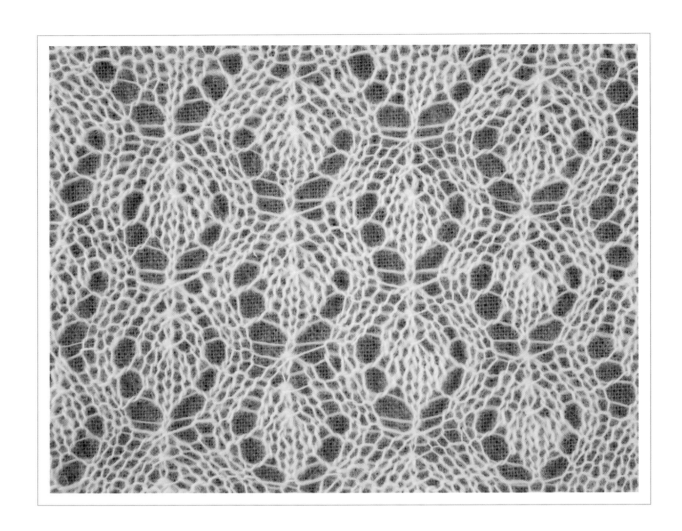

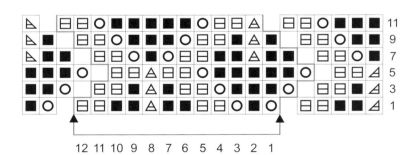

Leaf Pattern 3

Lehekiri 3

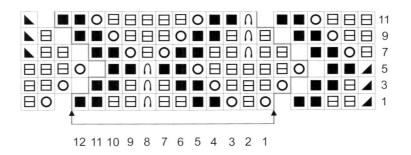

Leaf Pattern 4

Lehekiri 4

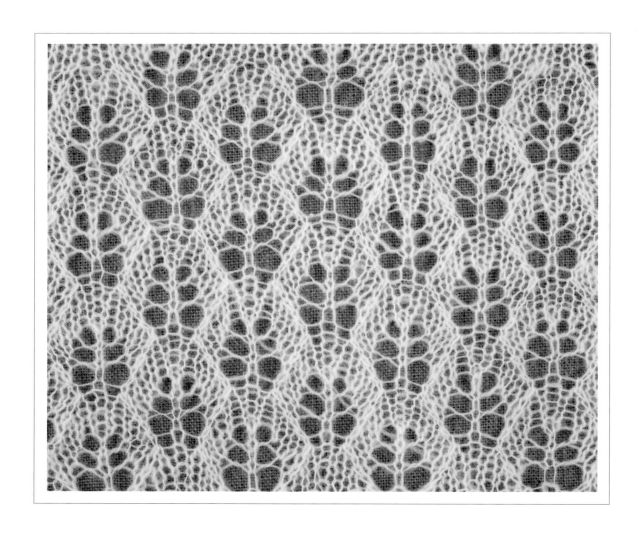

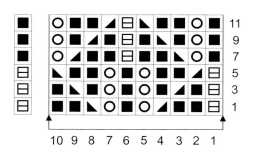

Half Leaf Pattern

Poollehekiri

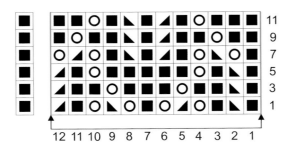

Five Leaf Pattern
Viislehekiri

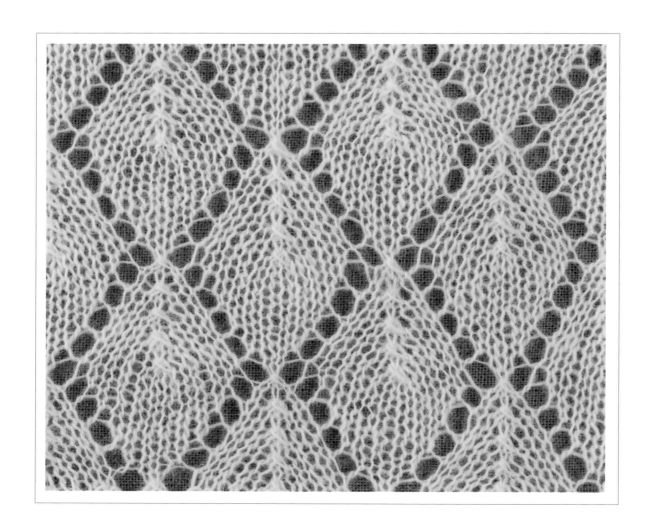

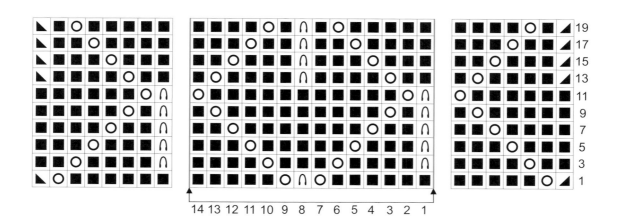

Big Leaf Pattern

Suur lehekiri

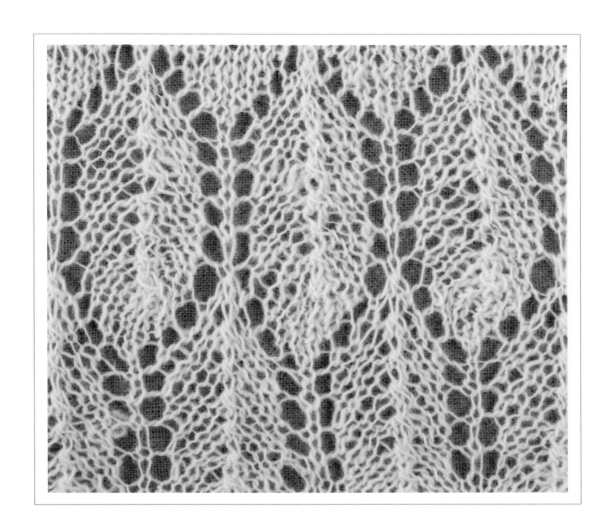

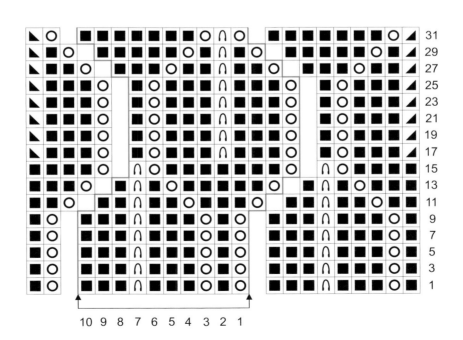

Alder Leaf Pattern
Lepalehekiri

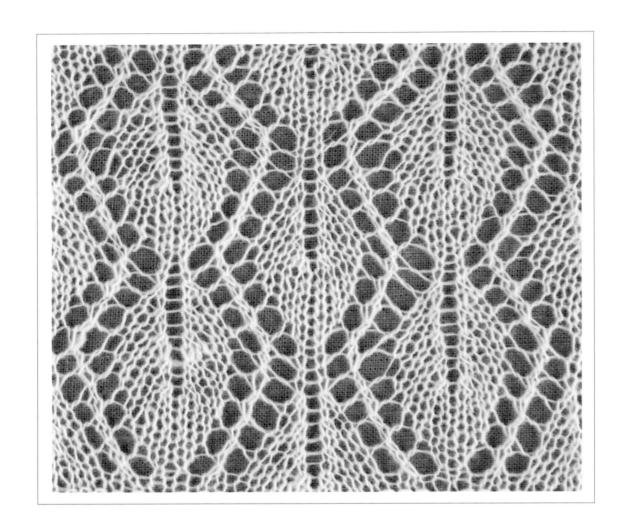

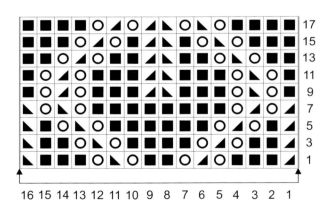

Paired Leaf Pattern
Paarislehekiri

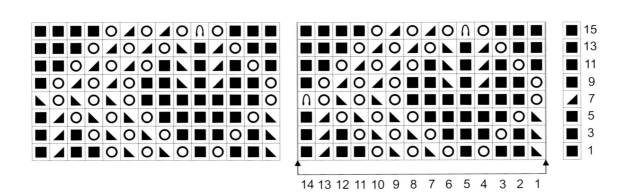

Leaf Pattern with Beetles
Sitikatega lehekiri

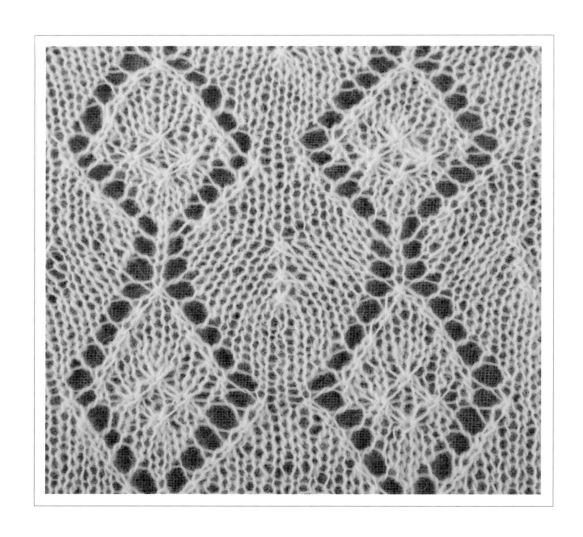

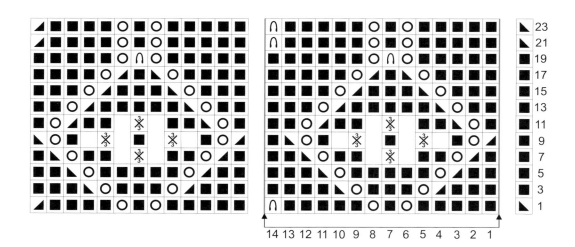

Wormeaten Leaf Pattern
Ussitanud lehekiri

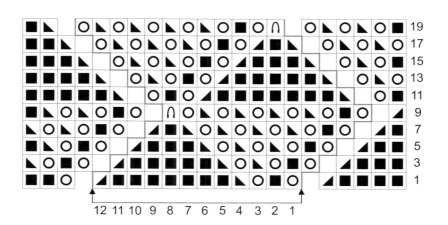

Dandelion Leaf Pattern

Võilillelehekiri

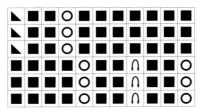

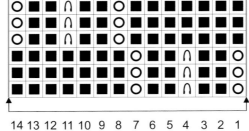

14 13 12 11 10 9 8 7 6 5 4 3 2 1

Maple Leaf Pattern

Vahtralehekiri

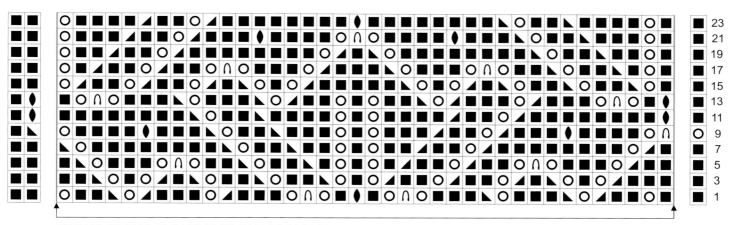

Lingonberry Leaf Pattern

Pohlalehekiri

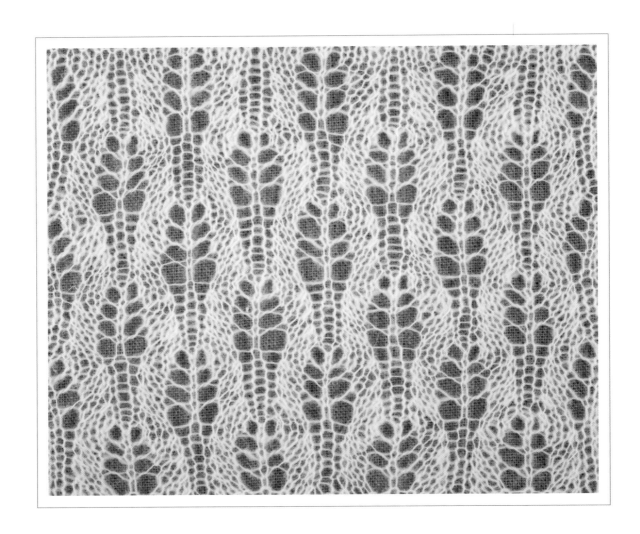

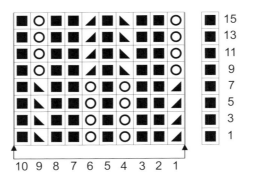

Lingonberry Leaf Pattern with Blossoms

Õitega pohlalehekiri

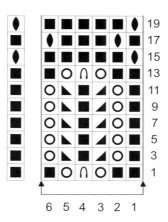

Quatrefoil Pattern
Õnnelehekiri

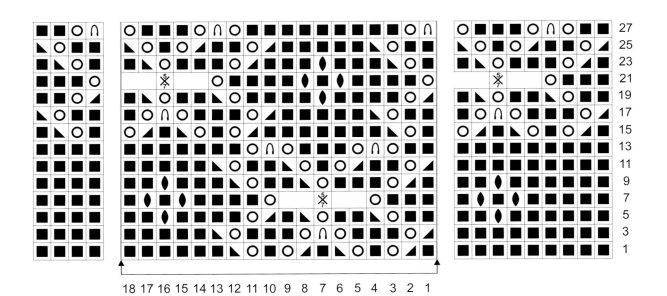

Quatrefoil with Stones Pattern

Kividega õnnelehekiri

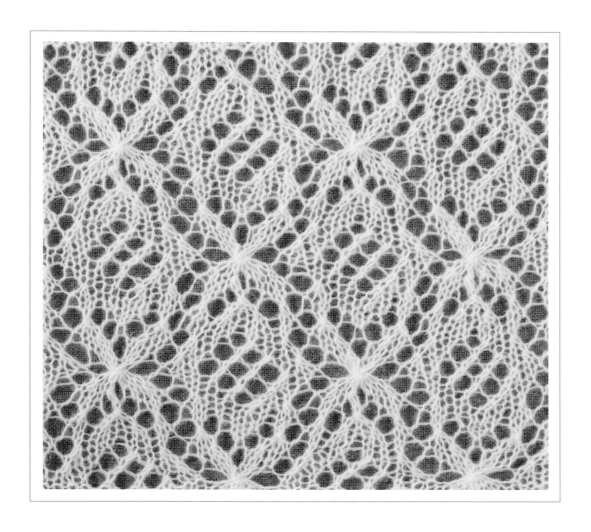

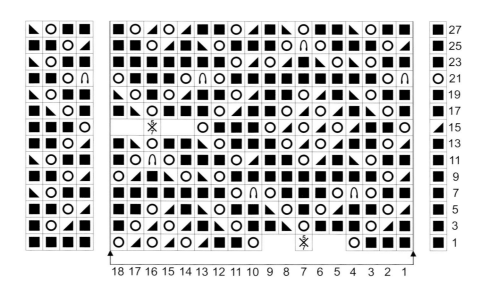

For me Haapsalu is the sea that meets you at every turn, scenic sunsets as well as lovely and lacy wooden houses in the old town. Haapsalu is a town that inspires you and gives you peace of mind at the same time.

Ingrid Danilov, mayor of Haapsalu

The shawl was knitted by Viivi Palmiste

Willow Leaf Pattern
Pajulehekiri

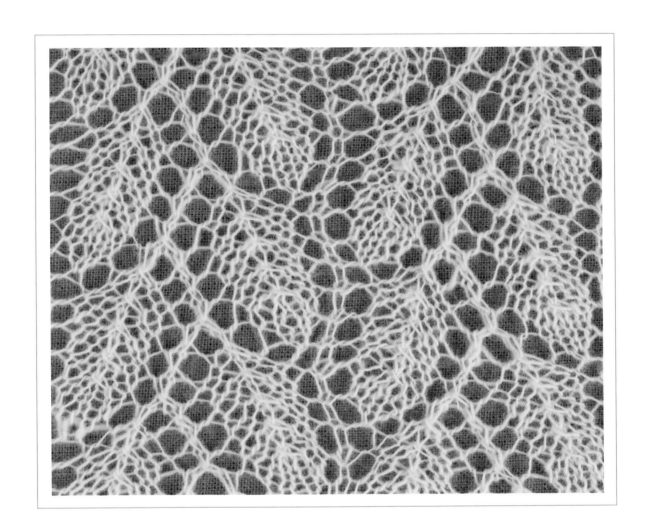

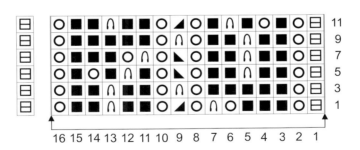

Willow Leaf Pattern with Nupps

Nuppudega pajulehekiri

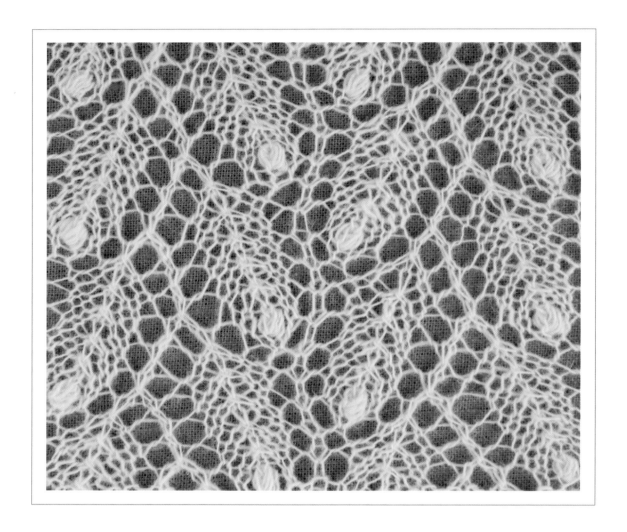

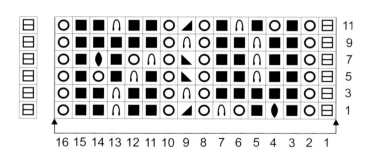

16 15 14 13 12 11 10 9 8 7 6 5 4 3 2 1

Small Willow Leaf Pattern
Väike pajulehekiri

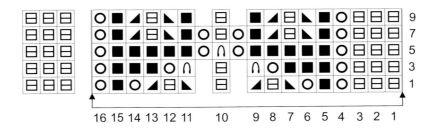

The shawl was knitted by Maiva Dunkel

Twig Patterns

This is also one of the oldest groups of stitch patterns. In Estonian the word *haga* comes from the word *hagu* meaning twigs for firewood or brushwood. In older literature it is also spelled *aga*. The pattern depicts a branched twig. The oldest twig patterns had no *nupps* but in developing the design many master knitters have added *nupps* or buds to the twigs.

Twig Pattern 1
Hagakiri 1

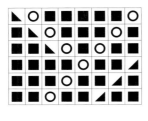 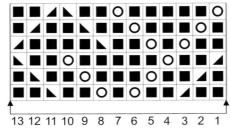 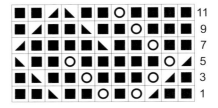

13 12 11 10 9 8 7 6 5 4 3 2 1

Twig Pattern 2
Hagakiri 2

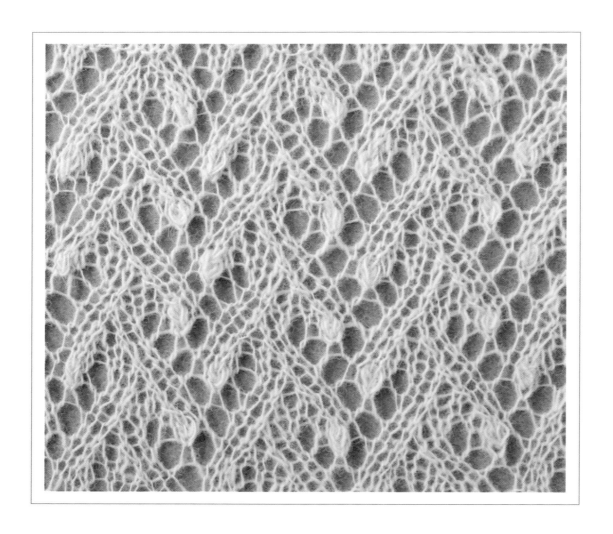

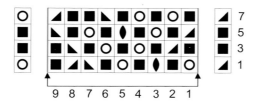

Twig Pattern 3

Hagakiri 3

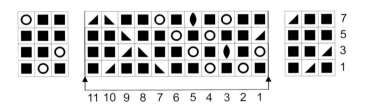

Twig Pattern 4
Hagakiri 4

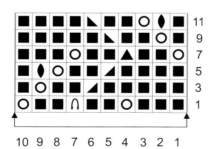

Twig Pattern with a Single Line 1

Ühe joonega hagakiri 1

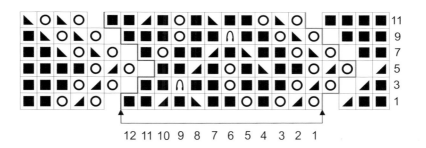

Twig Pattern with a Single Line 2

Ühe joonega hagakiri 2

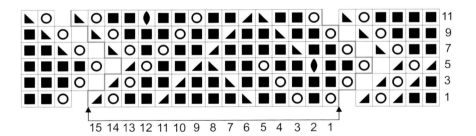

Twig Pattern with Two Lines

Kahe joonega hagakiri

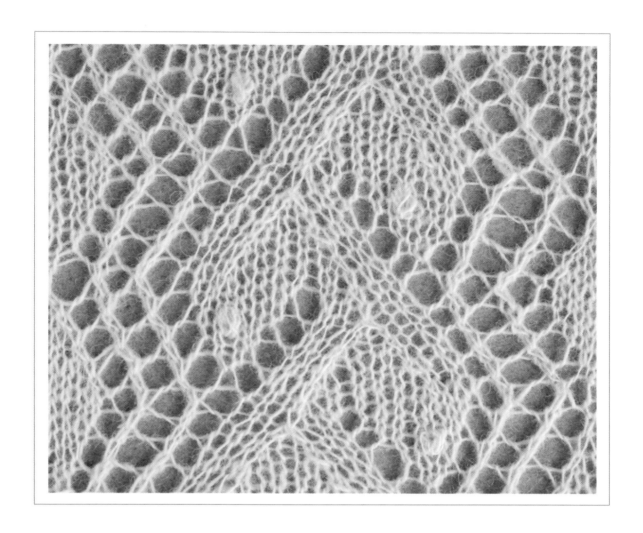

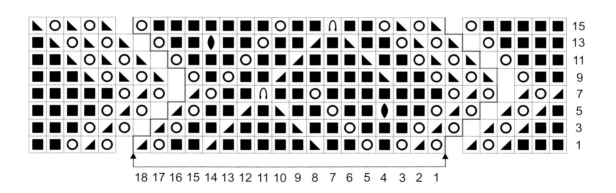

Simple Twig Pattern
Lihtne hagakiri

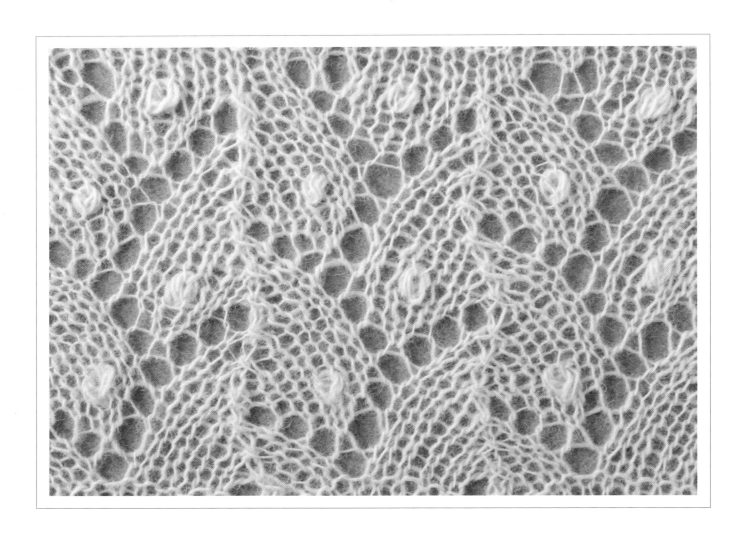

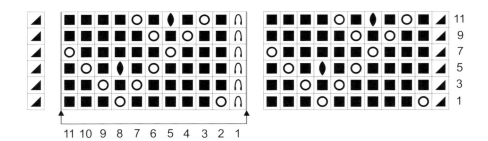

Lined Twig Pattern

Joonega hagakiri

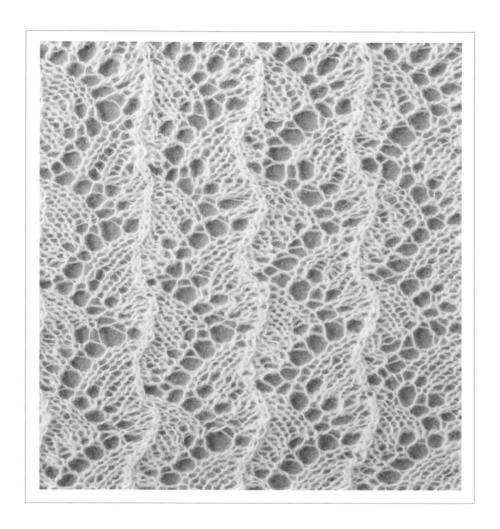

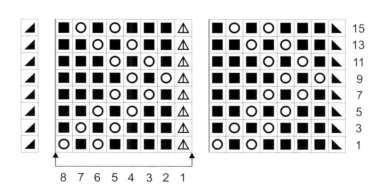

Slanting Twig Pattern 1
Viltune hagakiri 1

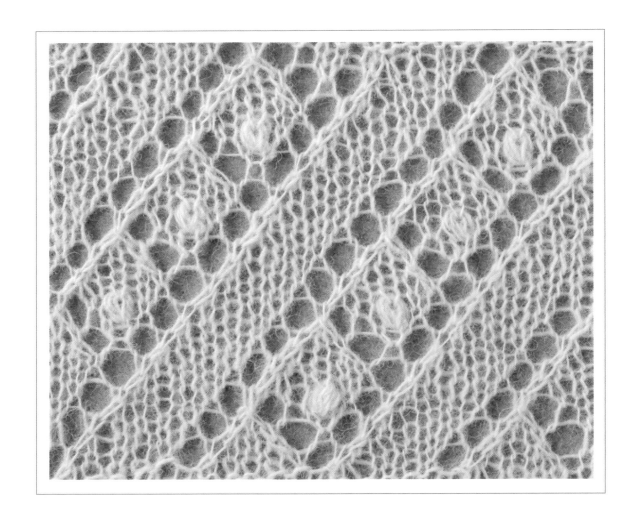

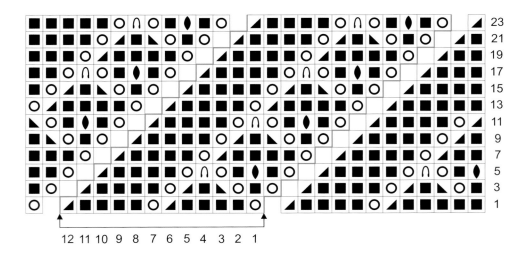

Slanting Twig Pattern 2
Viltune hagakiri 2

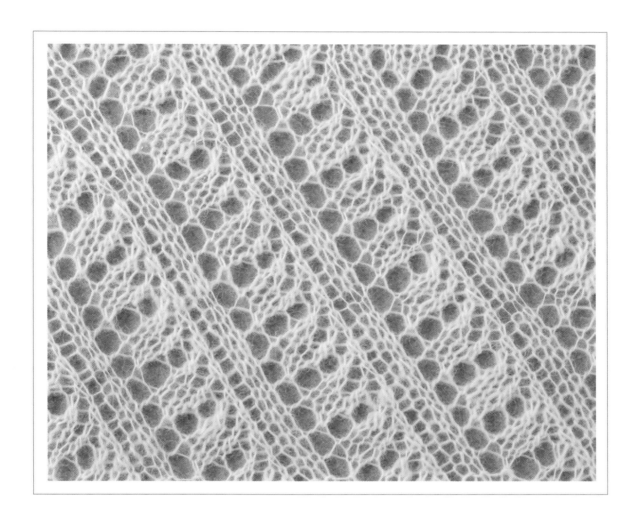

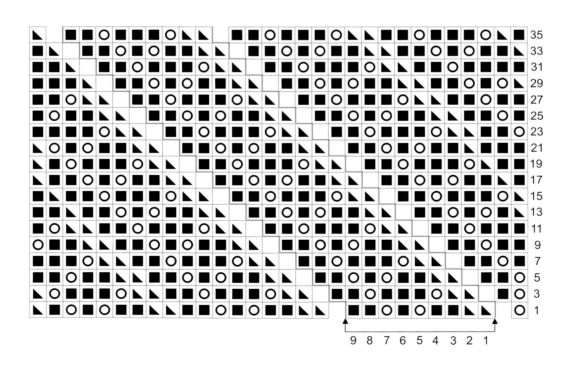

The shawl was knitted by Saima Tee

Peacock Tail Patterns

A peacock with its beautiful tail has inspired many lace knitters. Peacock tail patterns are one of the easiest to work and thus are perfectly suitable for beginners.

Peacock Tail Pattern 1
Vausabakiri 1

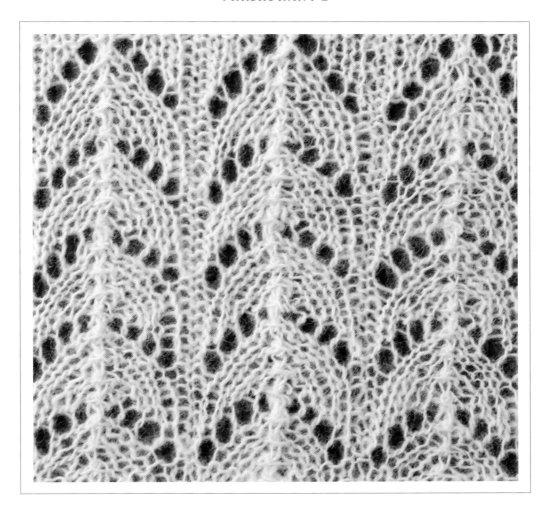

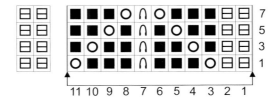

Peacock Tail Pattern 2

Vausabakiri 2

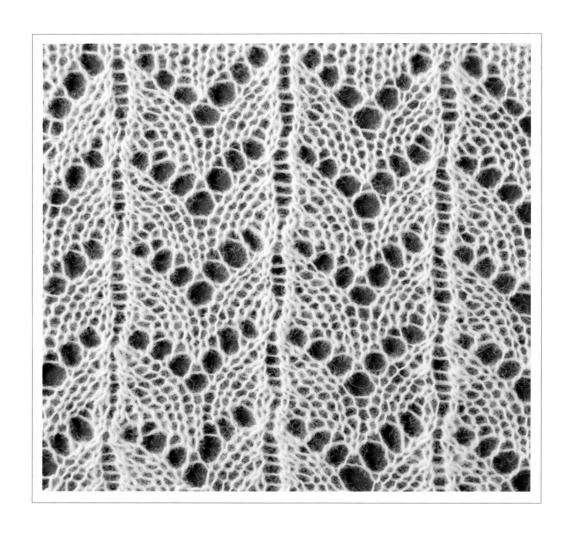

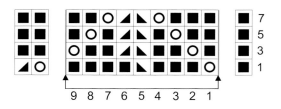

Peacock Tail Pattern 3
Vausabakiri 3

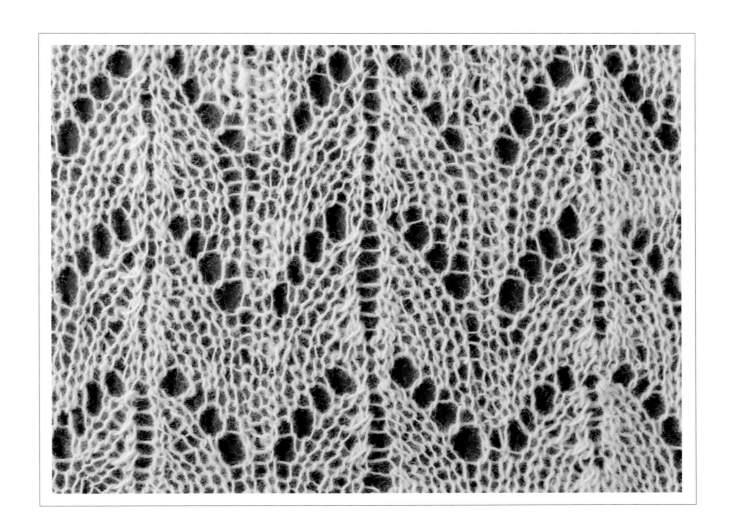

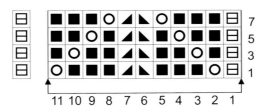

Peacock Tail Pattern 4
Vausabakiri 4

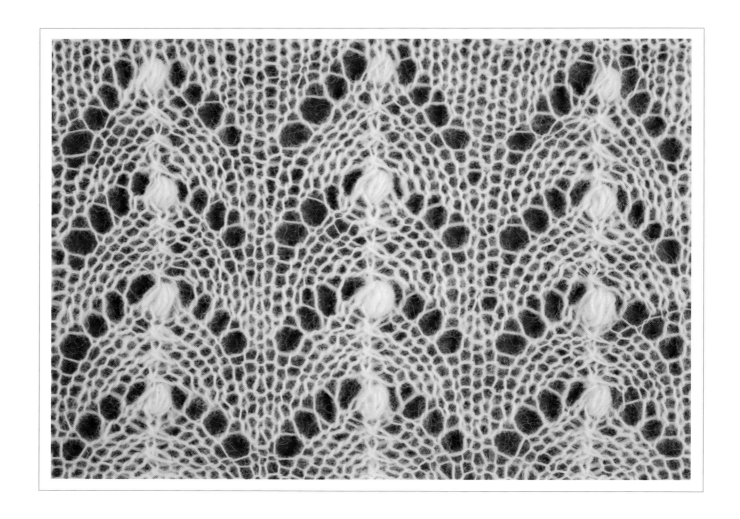

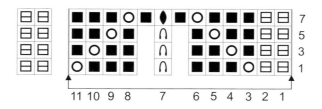

*In making a nupp for this pattern, increase 7 stitches,
on the wrong side row purl 9 stitches together (purl together the stitch preceding and following the nupp).*

Peacock Tail Pattern 5
Vausabakiri 5

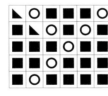
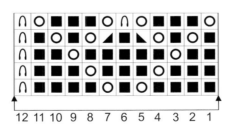
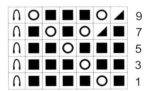

12 11 10 9 8 7 6 5 4 3 2 1

9
7
5
3
1

Peacock Tail Pattern 6
Vausabakiri 6

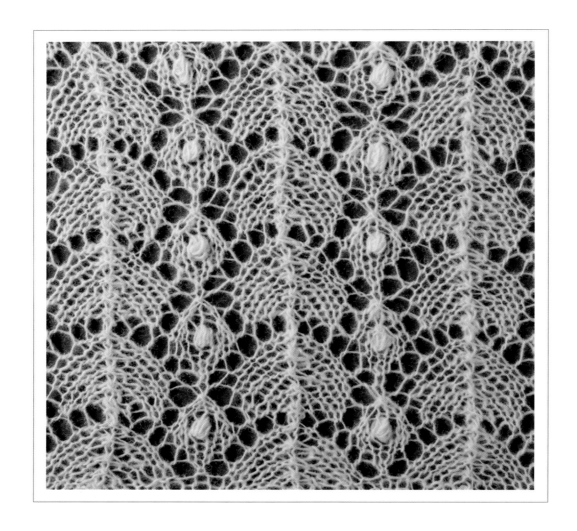

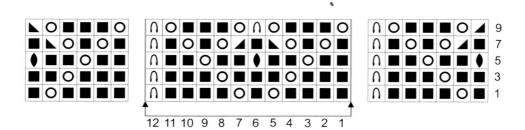

Peacock Tail Pattern 7
Vausabakiri 7

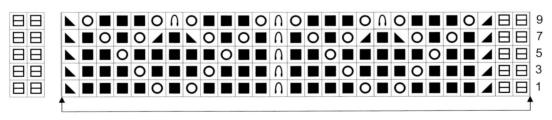

27 26 25 24 23 22 21 20 19 18 17 16 15 14 13 12 11 10 9 8 7 6 5 4 3 2 1

I have always been fond of beautiful and
practical things, something that pleases the eye
but can also be used.
Things which have been made with love and devotion,
using good material, and which are technically perfect.
I strive for this in my own work, too.
The Haapsalu shawl is delicate and feminine which
for me represents beauty, and it is warm
at the same time, or practical.
Thus, I wear it all through the winter and even in the
summer I poke it into my bag to throw it over my shoulders
while sitting out at night or after returning from a swim.

Liisu Arro, ceramist

The shawl was knitted by Laine Põldme

Paw Patterns

The shawl knitters have also found inspiration from animal tracks. Paw patterns are good for beginners as they are simple and do not include *nupps*.

Paw Pattern 1
Käpakiri 1

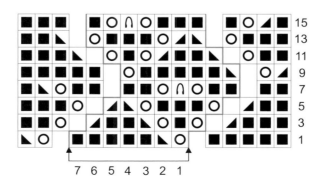

Paw Pattern 2

Käpakiri 2

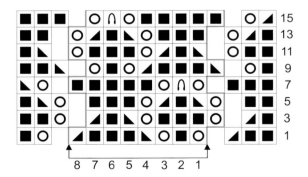

Paw Pattern 3

Käpakiri 3

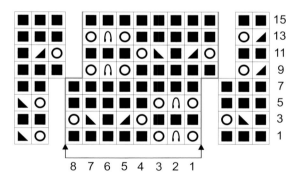

Paw Pattern 4
Käpakiri 4

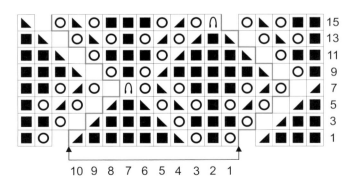

Cat's Paw Pattern

Kassikäpakiri

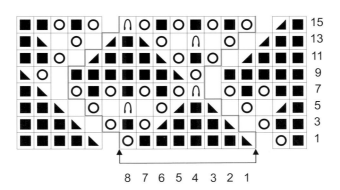

There is always wind in Haapsalu.
You get used to it, you knit together with it.

Aidi Vallik, writer

The shawl was knitted by Saima Tee

Head of Grain Patterns

Heads of grain ripening in the fields of Estonia inspired masters to create beautiful shawl patterns. This is a small group of patterns that continues to be to the liking of the master knitters.

Head of Grain Pattern 1
Viljapeakiri 1

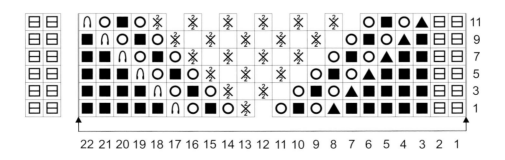

Head of Grain Pattern 2
Viljapeakiri 2

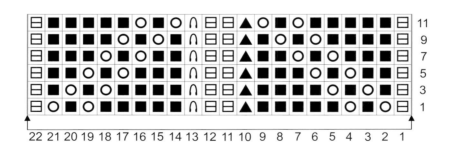

Head of Grain Pattern 3
Viljapeakiri 3

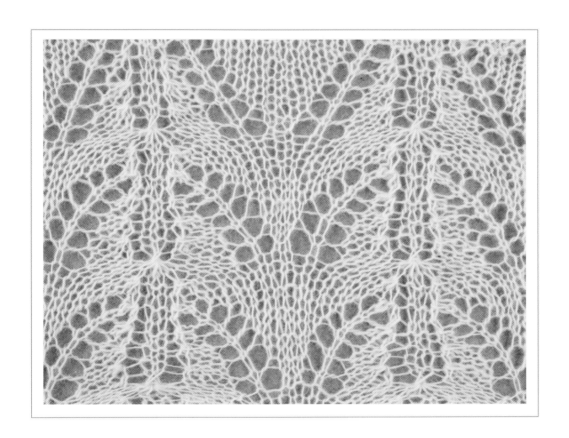

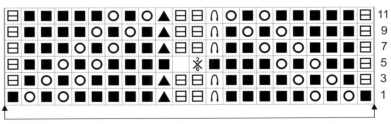

Head of Grain Pattern 4

Viljapeakiri 4

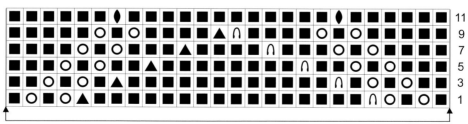

26 25 24 23 22 21 20 19 18 17 16 15 14 13 12 11 10 9 8 7 6 5 4 3 2 1

Head of Grain Pattern 5
Viljapeakiri 5

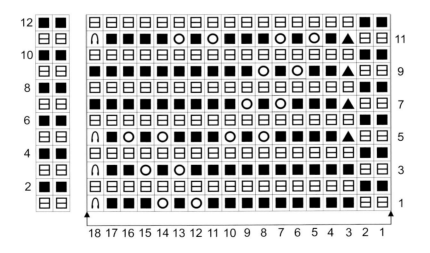

If even–numbered or wrong side rows are shown on the chart, begin reading the row from the side with the number, i.e. from the left. The symbols on this row indicate what you should actually do with the stitch, if the symbol is a knit, you should knit the stitch, if it is the symbol for purl, then purl it, etc.

Head of Grain Pattern with Flowers
Lilledega viljapeakiri

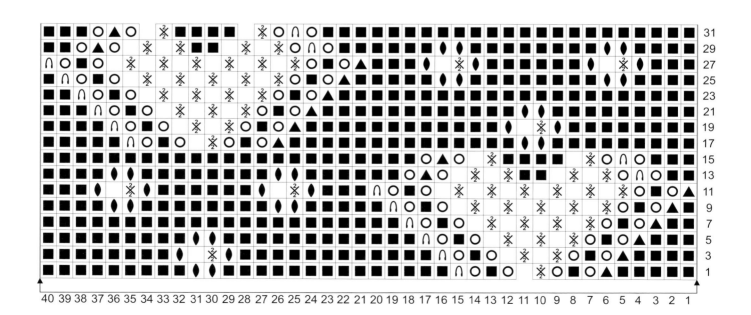

Head of Grain Pattern with a Flower
Lillega viljapeakiri

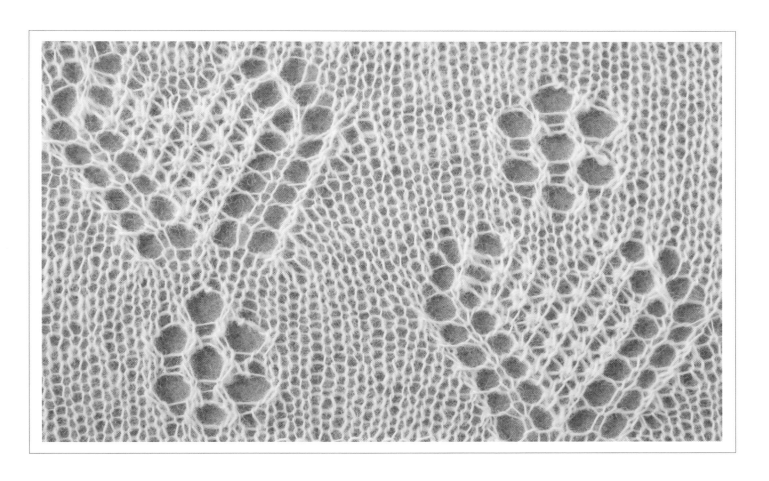

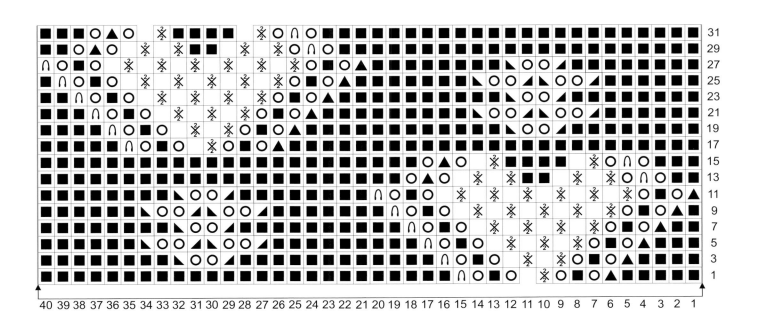

*U*nlike other parts of Estonia,
Haapsalu has such a pleasant climate that even the
magnolia successfully survives the winters here and gladdens her
mistress with beautiful blossoms in the early spring.

Liivia Leškin, fashion designer

The shawl was knitted by Helmi Mändla

Butterfly Patterns

The pattern reminds one of a butterfly stretching its wings. This is the only pattern of the Haapsalu shawls that uses cables.

Butterfly Pattern 1
Liblikakiri 1

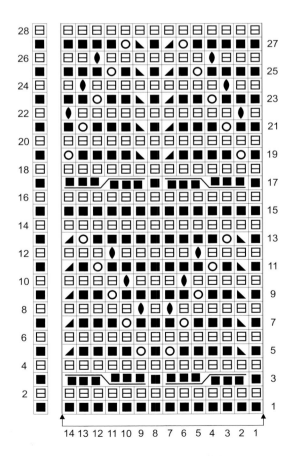

If even–numbered or wrong side rows are shown on the chart, begin reading the row from the side with the number, i.e. from the left. The symbols on this row indicate what you should actually do with the stitch, if the symbol is a knit, you should knit the stitch, if it is the symbol for purl, then purl it, etc.

Butterfly Pattern 2
Liblikakiri 2

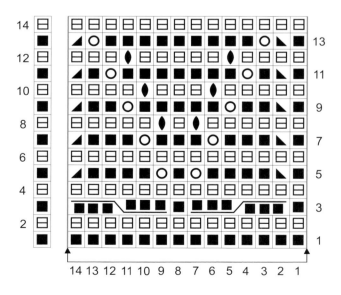

If even–numbered or wrong side rows are shown on the chart, begin reading the row from the side with the number, i.e. from the left. The symbols on this row indicate what you should actually do with the stitch, if the symbol is a knit, you should knit the stitch, if it is the symbol for purl, then purl it, etc.

Butterfly Pattern 3
Liblikakiri 3

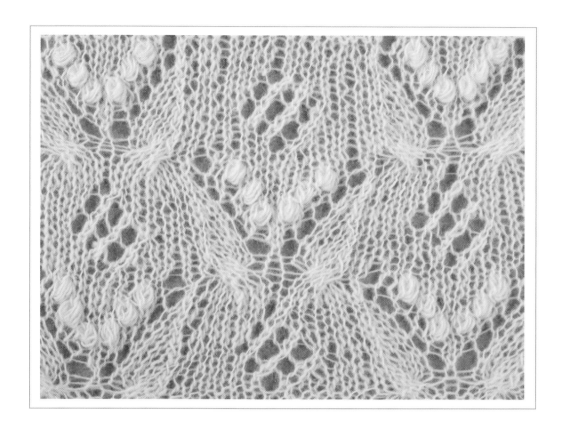

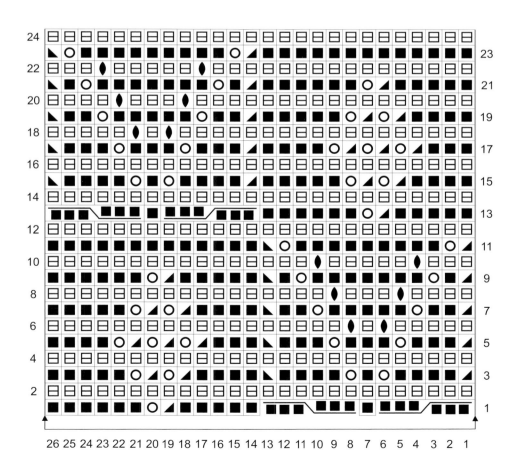

*W*earing an airy Haapsalu shawl on my shoulders
I feel as if I was covered with a protective magic veil.

Anni Arro, author of cookery books

The shawl was knitted by Siiri Reimann

Diamond Patterns

Diamond patterns are frequently used in more modern times. With the help of yarn overs and decreases characteristic of openwork patterns, it is easy to create interesting diamonds which form a beautiful geometric surface when worked into a shawl.

Cube Pattern with a Spruce
Kuusega kuubikukiri

Diamond Pattern 1
Rombikiri 1

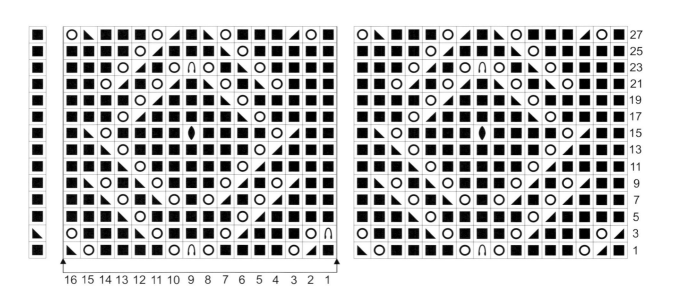

Diamond Pattern 2

Rombikiri 2

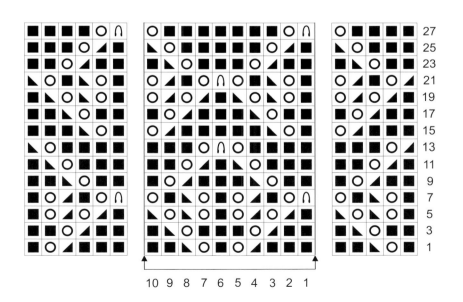

Diamond Pattern 3
Rombikiri 3

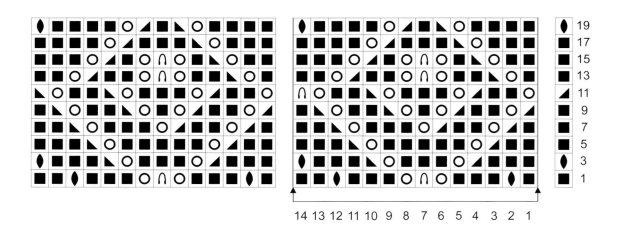

Diamond Pattern 4
Rombikiri 4

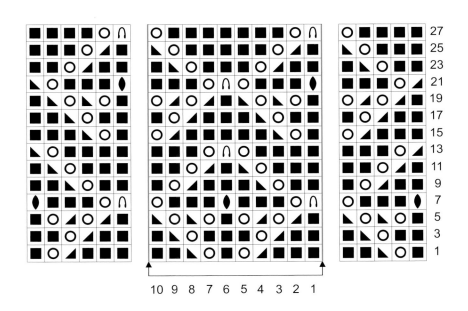

Diamond Pattern with a Flower
Lillega rombikiri

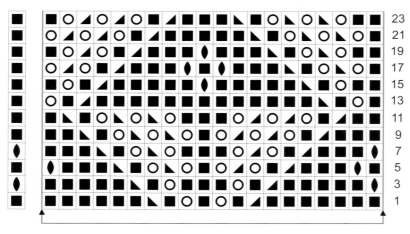

Diamond Pattern with Nupps
Nuppudega rombikiri

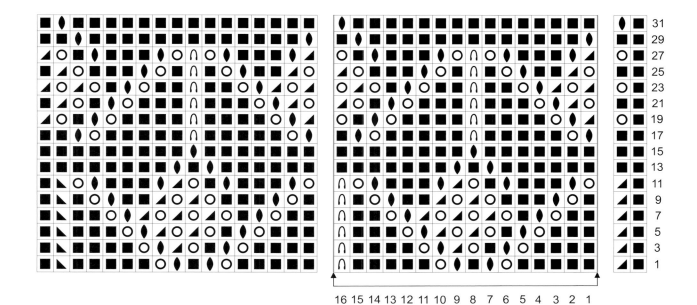

Cube Pattern
Kuubikukiri

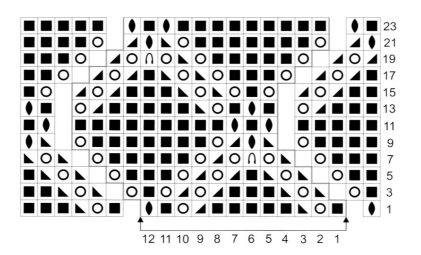

Diamond Spiral Pattern
Rombspiraalkiri

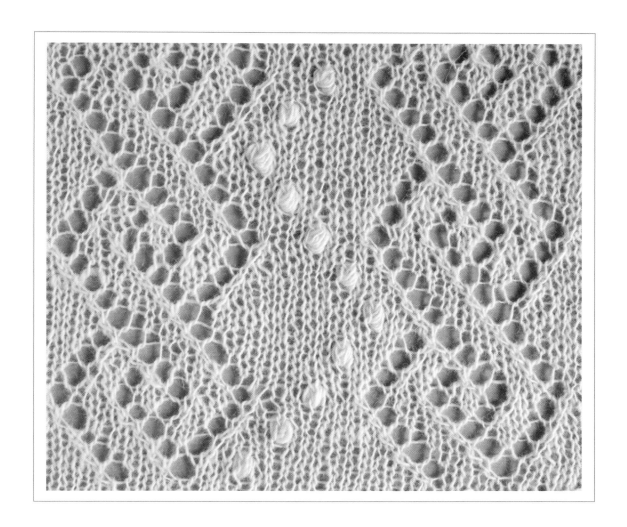

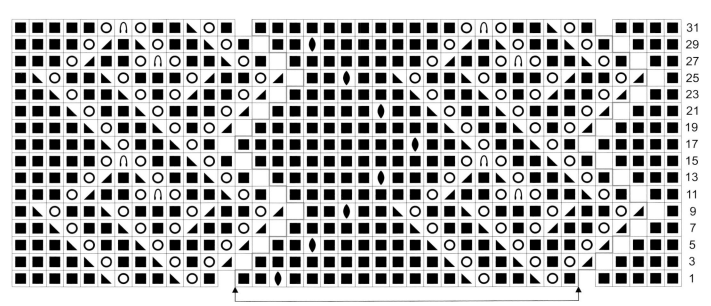

The shawl was knitted by Linda Elgas

Named Patterns

This group of named patterns includes shawl patterns from different times that are difficult to assign to some other group. This includes both newly designed and very old patterns that were knitted over one hundred years ago – money (*raha*), cookie (*prääniku*), wallpaper (*tapeedi*), crow's foot (*varesejala*) patterns, etc. This chapter also includes completely new patterns which have been created by the master knitters and, according to an old tradition, given names that pleased their creators, such as chick pattern (*tibukiri*), snowfall pattern (*lumesajukiri*), bindweed pattern (*kassitapukiri*) and water lily pattern (*vesiroosikiri*).

Money Pattern
Rahakiri

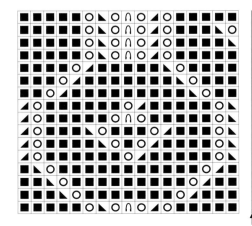

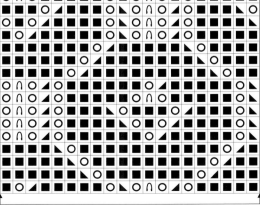

Wallpaper Pattern
Tapeedikiri

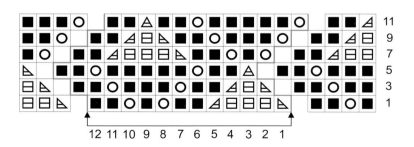

purl two stitches together through the back loops; a left-leaning decrease

Umbrella Pattern
Vihmavarjukiri

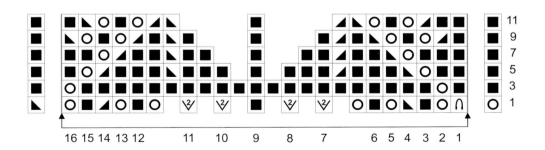

knit one stitch then knit into the back of the same stitch: two stitches from one

Cookie Pattern

Präänikukiri

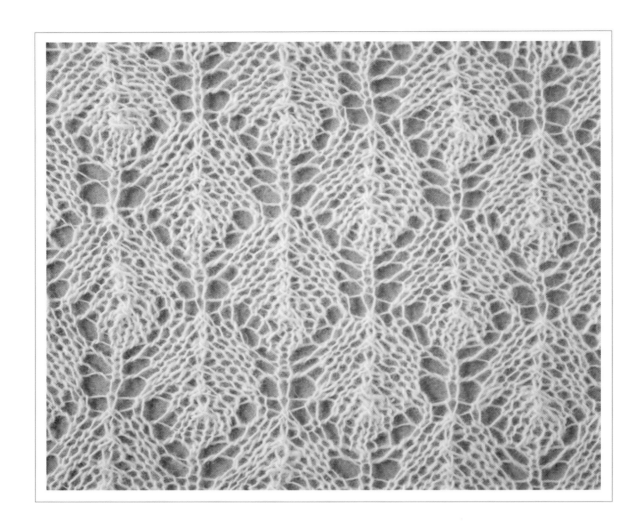

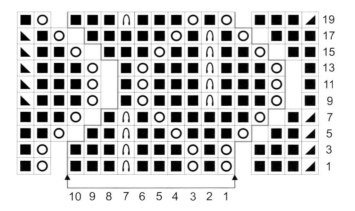

Crow's Foot Pattern
Varesejalakiri

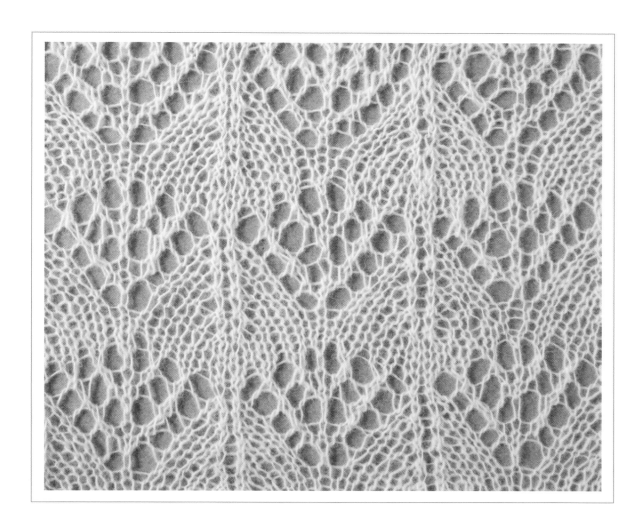

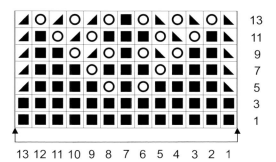

Ladybird Pattern
Lepatriinukiri

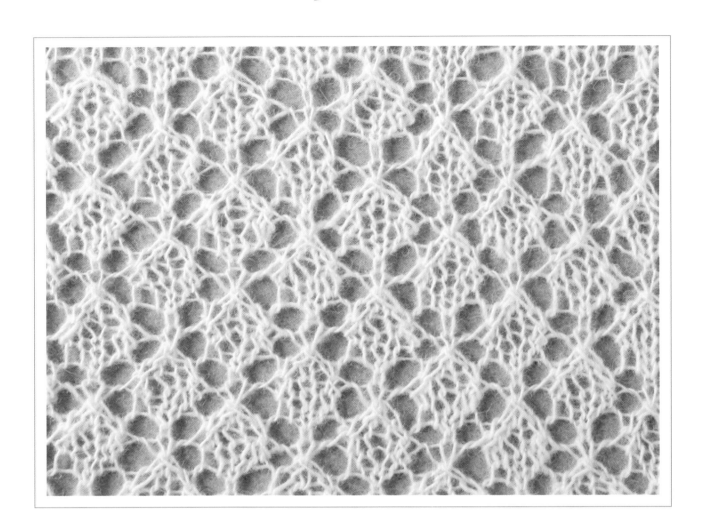

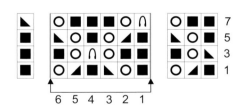

Milky Way Pattern

Linnuteekiri

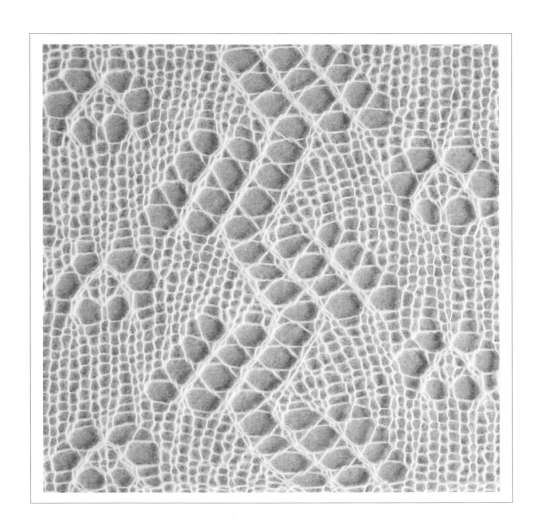

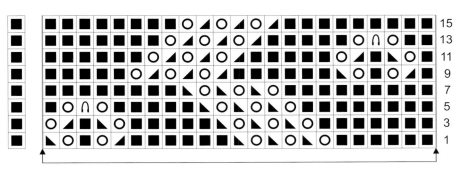

Flowers Pattern
Lilledekiri

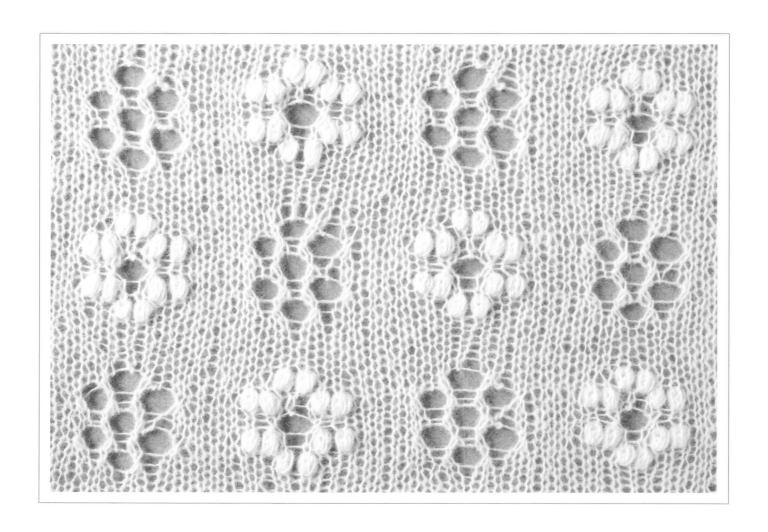

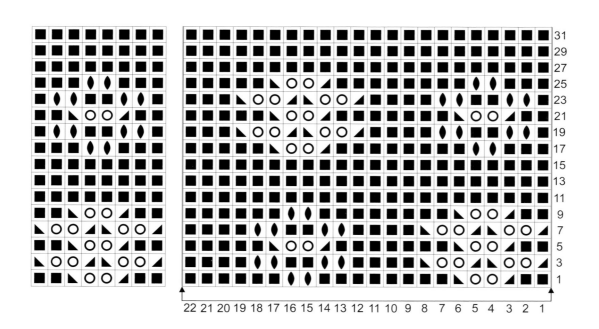

Water Lily Pattern

Vesiroosikiri

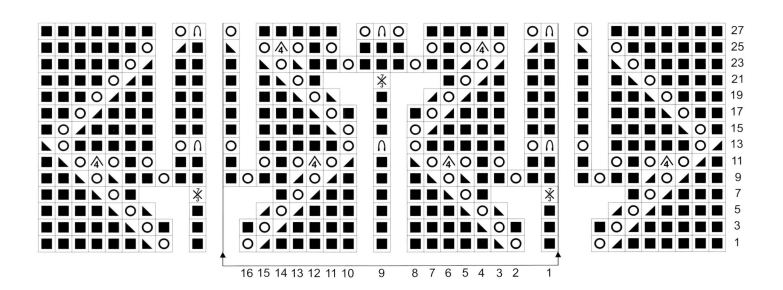

 knit four stitches together

The shawl was knitted by Helga Rüütel

Bindweed Pattern
Kassitapukiri

Chick Pattern
Tibukiri

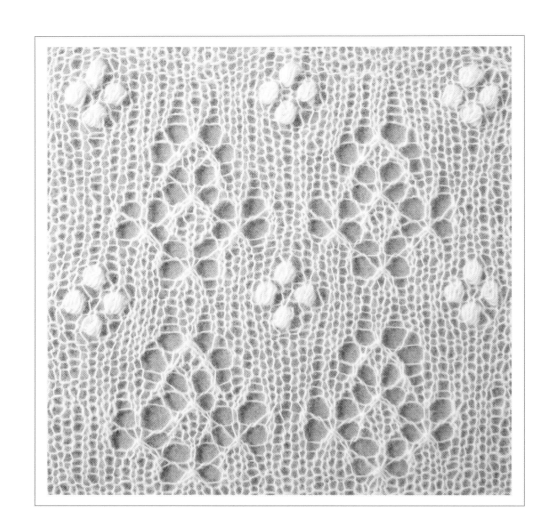

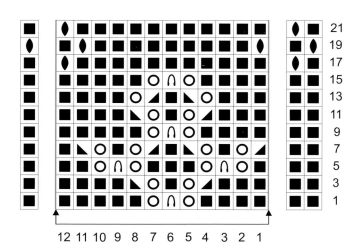

Flower Pattern

Lillekiri

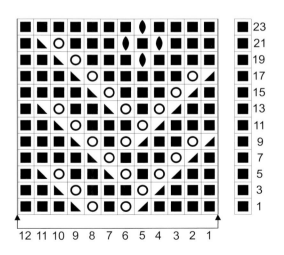

Snowdrift Pattern

Tuisukiri

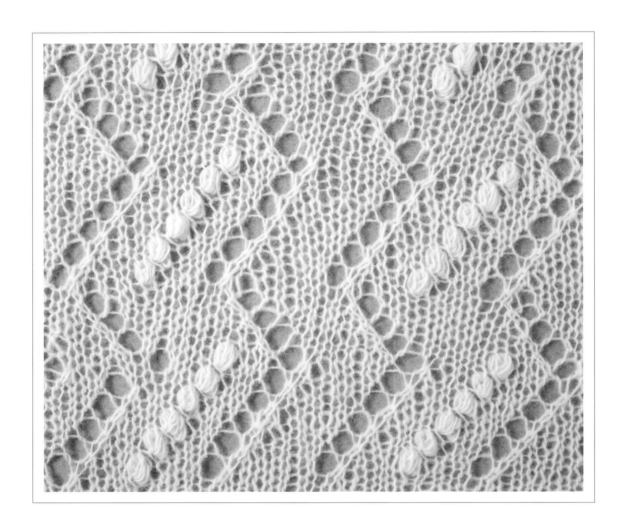

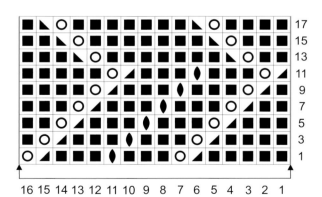

Snowfall Pattern

Lumesajukiri

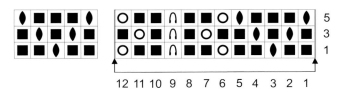

Wave Pattern

Merelainekiri

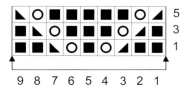

Lightning Pattern
Välgukiri

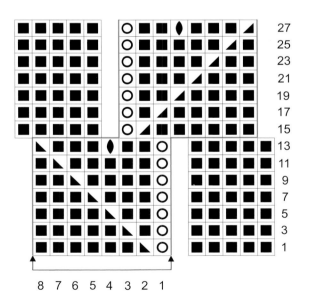

Stripe Pattern
Triibukiri

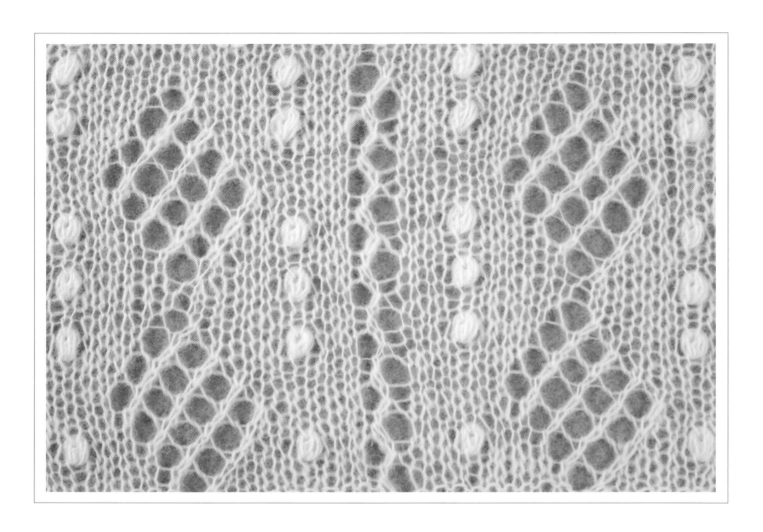

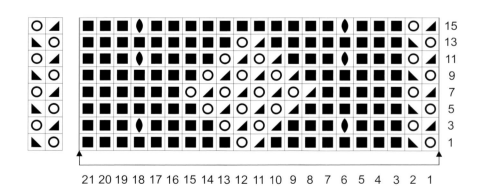

Tower Pattern
Tornikiri

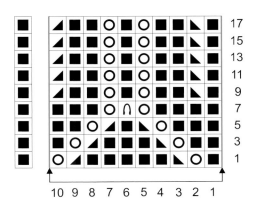

Linda Pattern
Lindakiri

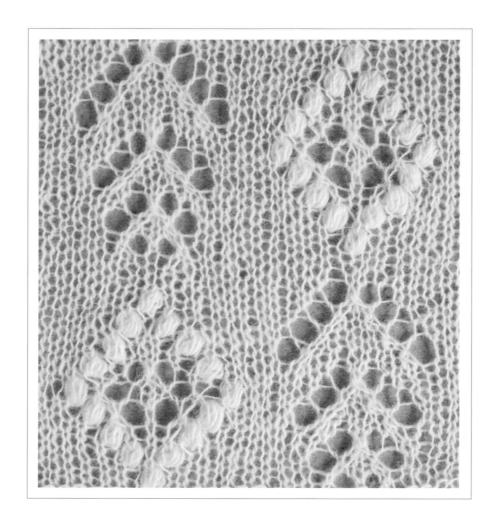

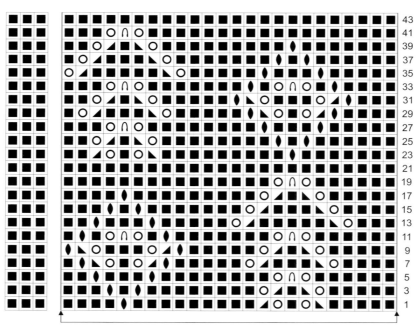

„The most Beautiful Shawl on Earth" Pattern

"Maailma ilusaim sallikiri"

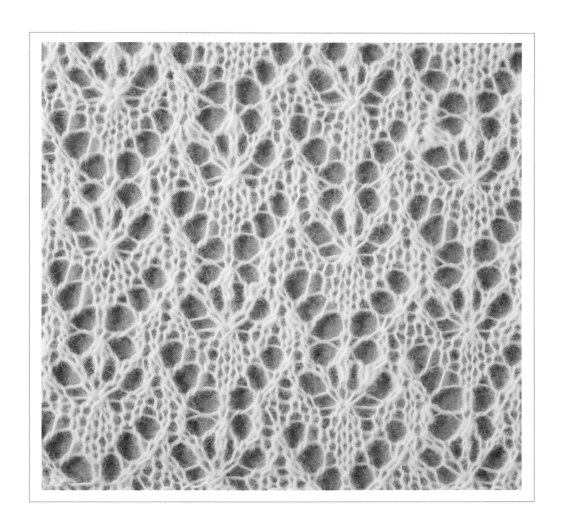

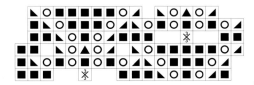
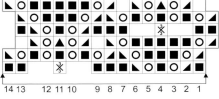
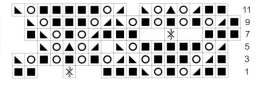

The shawl was bought in Estonia and taken to America. The pattern was duplicated there and one hundred shawls were ordered from Haapsalu. In America it was regarded as the most beautiful shawl on the earth.

Ornament Pattern 1
Ornamendikiri 1

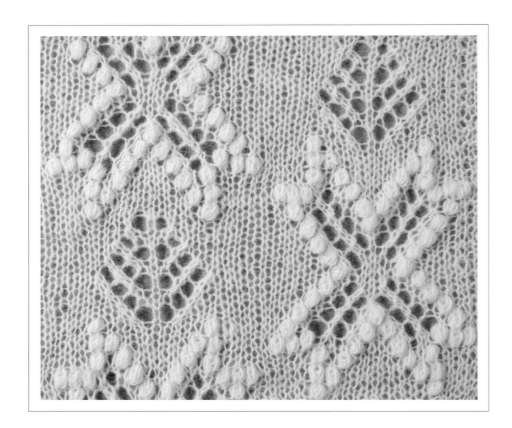

Ornament Pattern 2
Ornamendikiri 2

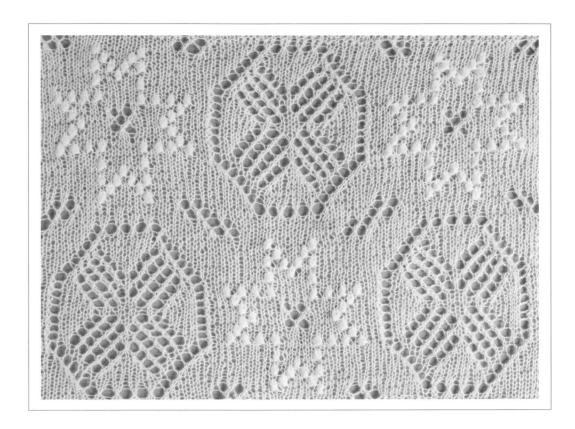

Lace Edges

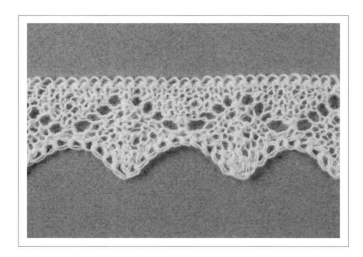

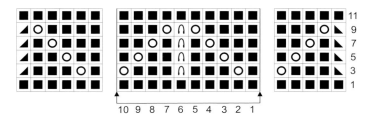

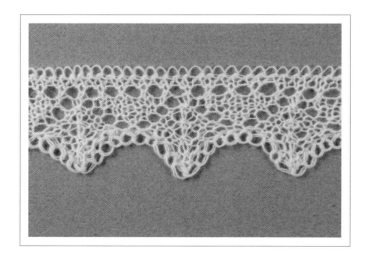

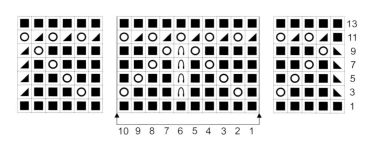

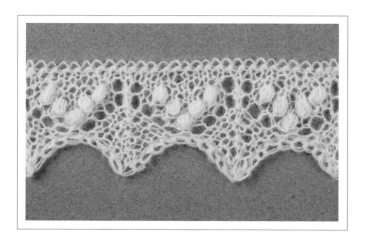

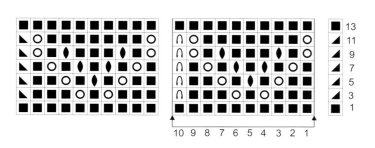

Lace Edges

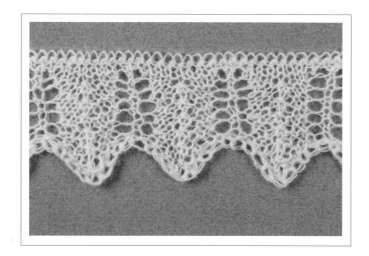
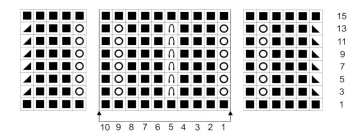

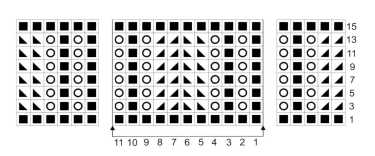

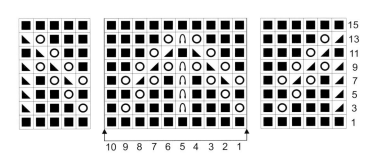

Lace Edges

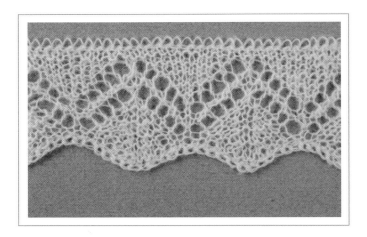

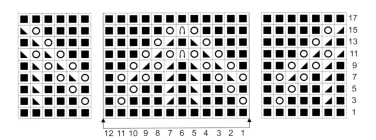

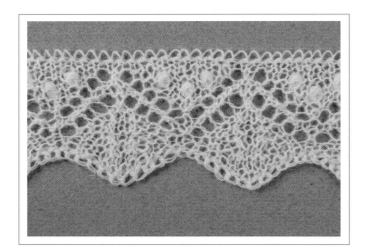

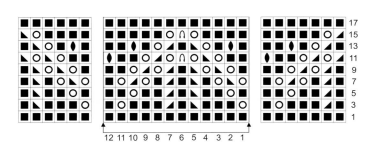

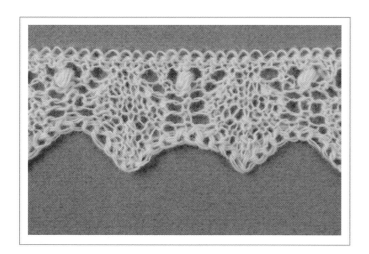

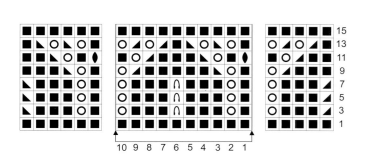

aapsalu is a good and quiet town. It wraps you in, just like this beautiful and delicate „armor".

Ilona Aasvere, singer and music teacher

Double lily of the valley shawl was knit by Aime Edasi